the INdigo CHILDREN

Other Hay House Titles of Related Interest

The Experience of God
How 40 Well-Known Seekers Encounter the Sacred,
by Jonathan Robinson

The Lightworker's Way
Awakening Your Spiritual Power to Know and Heal,
by Doreen Virtue, Ph.D.

The Power of Touch
The Basis for Survival, Health, Intimacy, and Emotional Well-Being,
by Phyllis K. Davis, Ph.D.

You Can Heal Your Life,
by Louise L. Hay

Your Personality, Your Health
*Connecting Personality with the Human Energy System,
Chakras, and Wellness,*
by Carol Ritberger, Ph.D.

(All of the above titles are available at your local bookstore,
or may be ordered by calling Hay House at 800-654-5126.)

———————————

Please visit the Hay House Website at: **www.hayhouse.com**
and
The Indigo Children Website at: **www.Indigochild.com**

the Indigo CHILDREN

The New Kids Have Arrived

Lee Carroll
and
Jan Tober

Hay House, Inc.
Carlsbad, California • Sydney, Australia

Published and distributed in the United States by:
Hay House, Inc., P.O. Box 5100, Carlsbad, CA 92018-5100
(800) 654-5126 • (800) 650-5115 (fax)

Editorial: Christine Watsky and Jill Kramer   *Design:* Renée G. Noël

The authors of this book do not dispense medical advice or prescribe the use of any technique as a form of treatment for physical or medical problems without the advice of a physician, either directly or indirectly. The intent of the authors is only to offer information of a general nature to help you in your quest for emotional and spiritual well-being. In the event you use any of the information in this book for yourself, which is your constitutional right, the authors and the publisher assume no responsibility for your actions.

Library of Congress Cataloging-in-Publication Data

Carroll, Lee.
    The Indigo Children : the new kids have arrived / Lee Carroll and Jan Tober.
        p.   cm.
    Includes bibliographical references.
    ISBN 1-56170-608-6
    1. Exceptional children.   2. Personality in children.   3. Color—
—Psychological aspects.   I. Tober, Jan (Jan M.)   II. Title.
HQ773.5.C36   1999
155.45—dc21   99–19532
                                                 CIP

ISBN 1-56170-608-6

04 03 02 01   18 17 16 15
1st printing, May 1999
15th printing, February 2001

Printed in Canada

Your children are not your children.

*They are the sons and the daughters of life's
longing for itself.*

They come through you but not from you,

And though they are with you, yet they belong not to you.

You may give them your love, but not your thoughts,

For they have their own thoughts.

You may house their bodies but not their souls,

*For their souls dwell in the house of tomorrow, which you
cannot visit, not even in your dreams.*

*You may strive to be like them, but seek not to
make them like you.*

*You are the bows from which your children as living
arrows are sent forth.*

Let your bending in the archer's hand be for gladness.

— Kahlil Gibran, The Prophet

For Jean Flores, United Nations worker,
who made her transition during the writing of this book.
She is now our angel on the other side,
still helping the children of the world.

"These kids can be very bright, very charming—and impossible to live with. They think of things that are fun and creative at the rate of about 10 per second. While you are trying to put out the fire they set toasting marshmallows on the stove, they are in the bathtub trying to see if goldfish will survive in hot water."
— Natasha Kern, mom, quoted by Nancy Gibbs in *Time* magazine.[1]

❧ Contents ❧

Introduction

As you begin to read this, you might be thinking, *What now, another "doom and gloom" book about how society is changing our kids?* No: This is perhaps the most exciting, albeit odd, change in basic human nature that has ever been observed and documented in any society with the tools to do so. We ask you to discern for yourselves as you read on.

Jan and I are national self-help lecturers and authors. In the last six years, we have traveled the world speaking in front of large and small groups alike. We have dealt with all ages and many cultures representing many languages. My boys are grown and left the nest long ago. Jan never had children, but somehow felt that someday she would be working with them (she was right). Of our six previously published books, none are about children because our work does not focus there. How is it, therefore, that we are authoring a book on this very subject?

When you are counselors and you spend close personal time with people, you cannot help but notice certain emerging patterns of human behavior, which then become staples of your work. Our work, like that of Louise Hay, who published this book, is about self-empowerment and the raising of self-esteem. It enables people to hope, giving them the power to lift themselves above the level of who they "thought" they were. It also involves spiritual healing (not religion), and encourages self-examination for the purpose of finding the "God within" first, before searching for any outside source. It speaks of self-healing, as well as independence from worry, in a changing and worry-prone world. It's tremendously rewarding work—but it makes us notice things.

Some years ago, people started to talk about specific troubles with their kids. So what else is new? Children are often the greatest blessing in a life, and also the greatest challenge. Many books have been written about good parenting and child psychology, but what we noticed was different.

We started hearing more and more about a new kind of child, or at least a new kind of problem for the parent. The difficulties were odd in nature, in that they represented an interchange between adult and child that was unexpected and seemingly atypical of what our generation had experienced. We ignored it until we started hearing it from the professionals who deal specifically with children. They were also reporting similar challenges. Many were exasperated and at their wit's end. Day-care workers all over the nation, some of whom had worked in their profession for over 30 years, were also telling us the same kind of stories about how things were somehow different with the kids. Then we saw something that was horrifying. When these "new" problems became acute, there was an overwhelming propensity to solve the issue by legally drugging the child!

At first, we assumed that this was a cultural attribute, reflecting a changing America. Part of our great American temperament is that we are flexible and go through remarkable changes, as no other country can, while keeping a stable governmental base. Ask any schoolteacher these days, and they will tell you that our educational system really needs an overhaul. It's probably time, but this isn't revolutionary news and did not inspire us to write this book.

Jan and I work with *individual* issues and stay away from politics or even environmental "causes." It's not that we aren't interested, but rather that our focus as counselors and lecturers is truly about helping men and women personally (even though we often speak to them in large groups). Our premise has always been that each balanced human who has a positive outlook and exudes well-being is able to make whatever changes necessary in a very powerful way. In other words, even vast sweeping social change has to start inside the mind and heart of one person at a time.

Additionally, we assumed that even if there were great changes going on with the kids, professionals and researchers would communicate about this within their industry—that the "pros" would also be observing this event. Years ago, we expected to see reports and articles on "attributes of the new kids" in elementary educational and day-care periodicals. It didn't happen— at least not on a scale that would draw much attention, and not in a way for parents to be helped or informed.

Because it didn't happen, we were reinforced in our original notion that our own observations were probably not as widespread as we had thought, and again, children are not our focus. It took several years for us to change our minds and decide that someone had to at least assemble the information and report it, no matter how strange it seemed. It was there!

As you can see, a number of factors brought about this book, which you should know about before you blindly take our word for something that is going to fall into the category of "happening all around us—but unexplainable."

We have now realized the following:

1. This is not an American phenomenon. We have now personally seen it on three continents.

2. It seems to go far beyond cultural barriers (encompassing multiple languages).

3. It has escaped mainstream attention due to the fact that it is just too "weird" to consider in the paradigm of human psychology, which smugly considers humanity as a static, unchanging model. As a rule, society tends to believe in evolution, but only in the past tense. The thought that we might be seeing a new human consciousness slowly arriving on the planet *now*—manifested in our children—goes way beyond established conservative thought.

4. The phenomenon is increasing—more reports continue to surface.

5. It has been around long enough that many professionals are beginning to observe it.

6. There are some emerging answers to the challenges.

For all these reasons, we are stepping out on a limb and giving you the best information we can about what we have observed on a subject that is undoubtedly controversial for many reasons. As far as we know, this is the first book entirely dedicated to the Indigo Child. While reading this, many will relate to what is presented, and we fully expect the subject to be explored more fully in the future by those more qualified.

The Goal of This Book

This book is written for parents. It's a beginning report, and is not the "end all" of the Indigo Child subject. It is presented to help you with your family, and to give you information for practical application should you identify with any of the subject matter. We ask for your discernment in all that is put forward. We would not be publishing this compilation unless we were certain that many of you will indeed find it revealing and helpful. This book has been assembled mainly through the encouragement, and sometimes pleading, of hundreds of parents and teachers that we have spoken to around the world.

The Method

We thought about how wonderful it would be to give you story after story from parents about their Indigo Children—there are so many. But these are just stories, and don't validate behavior in a way that researchers (or logical thinkers) can relate to. Therefore, we decided to use our international base of contacts to collect a series of reports, comments—and yes, a few stories—by accredited children's workers, teachers, Ph.D.'s, M.D.'s, and authors all over the country. As you continue reading, you will find that we have tried our best to bring validation in a real-world way to something that we have observed in a nonscientific way through our work. We have also included some case histories in the areas of the book where we felt a scientific approach would be best. Since we personally have not done accredited research into this area, we felt that the reports and findings of the professionals who have contributed here would help validate the premise we are presenting.

Organization

We chose a structure that would be as helpful as possible. This introduction will help you get to know us, and hopefully will establish the fact that we are indeed interested in your children!

Chapter 1 is our attempt to identify the attributes of these children, and introduces some of the contributors and participants whom you will hear from throughout some of the other chapters as well.

Chapter 2 concerns itself immediately with what to do with an Indigo Child. In many books, this practical chapter would be the book's conclusion, but our subsequent chapters get into some medical and/or esoteric subjects that should stand alone in their revelations. Therefore, the first two chapters contain answers and practical information that also can stand alone should you choose not to continue delving into deeper studies. This chapter also discusses the educational process and alternate schooling for Indigos.

Chapter 3 is about the spiritual aspects of the Indigo Child phenomenon. This isn't about religion, but rather a report on some very unusual attributes, common to the children, which *must* be included in this book. They seem to spiritually "know who they are," and report it to their parents very early! Can we really leave this out?

Chapter 4 is about how these children are being diagnosed medically. Not all Indigo Children have big psychological problems, but when they do, they often end up being diagnosed as ADD or ADHD (Attention Deficit Disorder and Attention Deficit Hyperactive Disorder, respectively). Now, not all ADD children are Indigo; however, would you like to know some alternate methods of treatment for ADD that *work*? We have tried to give you some in chapter 4—traditional and nontraditional—with case histories to match. This is an attempt to get children off of drugs that sedate them, and to give parents some alternatives to try.

Here is a sobering thought: If you are a parent with a sedated child, you might feel that Ritalin is a real solution. The child behaves better, seems calmer, and things are more stable in the family and at school—whew! Ritalin, however, puts the child into a holding pattern of behavior—which the child may even like. But later in life, when the stopper comes out of the bottle (when they come off the drug), the bubbles inside may still cause some kind of explosion. In retrospect, after growing up, they may feel that they lost part of their childhood in a murky remembrance unconnected to their true self. Ritalin often postpones the real issue of growing up, and the wisdom that comes with it—learning how society works. This is documented.

There actually might be a method to help your child without using Ritalin, represented by some alternate treatment. An open mind might help, and we present some people with very impressive credentials and good results who would love to assist in this area.

Chapter 5 brings you some messages from actual Indigos. Included are writings from a few grown, or almost grown, Indigo Children. It's their perspective, looking back at their upbringing. Believe us, they know they are different! These writings are quite profound.

Chapter 6, the summary, presents you with short messages from each of us.

The Contributors

Each time we introduce a contributor, we will include their credentials. Full information can be found in the back about them as well as their organizations. We encourage you to write, e-mail, or call them if you have questions or wish to obtain their books or products. We have also tried to give you their Internet addresses if they represent organizations. If they do not have e-mail or Internet addresses and there is nothing else listed for them, go ahead and write to them in care of Hay House, using the address in the back. If you do, be sure to mention this book title, and they will forward your requests to whomever you are writing. You can also write us with questions, but we do not feel that we are experts. We are reporters here, and have simply served to compile a group of more qualified workers to help identify and deal with the Indigo subject. Probably, we will simply forward your questions to the appropriate contributor.

The References

Each time there is further information available for the subject at hand, you will see a small superscript number in the text. This number refers to an endnote—look in the back of the book for references to other books, products, and organizations.

chapter one

What Is an Indigo Child?

What is an Indigo Child? And why do we call them *Indigo*? First, the definition: an Indigo Child is one who displays a new and unusual set of psychological attributes and shows a pattern of behavior generally undocumented before. This pattern has common unique factors that suggest that those who interact with them (parents, in particular) change their treatment and upbringing of them in order to achieve balance. To ignore these new patterns is to potentially create imbalance and frustration in the mind of this precious new life. The subject of this chapter is to identify, qualify, and validate the attributes of an Indigo Child.

There seem to be several kinds of Indigos, and we will describe them later in this chapter, but in the following list we can give you some of the most common behavioral patterns. Do these fit anyone you know?

Here are ten of the most common traits of Indigo Children:

1. They come into the world with a feeling of royalty (and often act like it).

2. They have a feeling of "deserving to be here," and are surprised when others don't share that.

3. Self-worth is not a big issue. They often tell the parents "who they are."

4. They have difficulty with absolute authority (authority without explanation or choice).

5. They simply will not do certain things; for example, waiting in line is difficult for them.

6. They get frustrated with systems that are ritual-oriented and don't require creative thought.

7. They often see better ways of doing things, both at home and in school, which makes them seem like "system busters" (nonconforming to any system).

8. They seem antisocial unless they are with their own kind. If there are no others of like consciousness around them, they often turn inward, feeling like no other human understands them. School is often extremely difficult for them socially.

9. They will not respond to "guilt" discipline ("Wait till your father gets home and finds out what you did").

10. They are not shy in letting you know what they need.

We will examine some of these traits later in a closer way, but next we wish to let you know why these children are called *Indigo*.

Throughout the history of psychology, there have been systems of grouping human behavior. Indeed, often we all seem to fall into "clumps" of behavior patterns, sometimes fun to read about and identify. These groupings try to identify and correlate human actions in many different ways—undoubtedly searching for some formula that neatly fits everyone into a slot of some kind, helping those who deal with the study of the human mind. Some of these systems are ancient; some are very new.

Right away, we would like to turn to a psychiatrist for a very brief validation of this fact, so we can begin on a solid academic footing. **Richard Seigle** is not only a practicing doctor, but is also involved in human and spiritual studies with native healing.

Human Categorizing Systems
Richard Seigle, M.D.

Throughout the history of Western civilization, we have had a strong need to explore, define, and judge. As we discovered new lands and peoples on Earth, our first thoughts were, *Who is like us and who is not,* and *What can we take?* Those people who were not like us in terms of color, belief, culture, and language were considered inferior throughout much of our history.

In scientific terms, we tried to categorize people by the shape of their heads, skin color, IQ, and so on. Anthropologists and psychologists have spent years evaluating how we think, feel, and act. Here are some examples of various categorization systems:

- **Intelligence tests,** such as Wechsler (WAIS) and Stanford-Binet Personality.

- **Personality tests,** such as MMPI, MCMI, Type A, and Type B.

- **Projective personality assessments,** such as Rorschach, TAT, and SCT.

- **Memory tests,** such as WMS and Bender.

- **Specific psychological factors.** Factors such as the following have sometimes been used as a basis for grouping human behavior: family structure and customs; culture; dreams; self-psychology; bonding and attachment; myths; religion; conscious and unconscious motivation and thoughts.

- **Recognized psychiatric theorists** such as the following used various systems of personality typing: Freud, Jung, Adler, Berne, Fromm, Kernberg, Klein, Maslow, Peris, Reich, Rogers, Skinner, and Sullivan.

Gandhi said, "Our ability to reach unity in diversity will be the beauty and test of our civilization." The end of this millennium signals a higher consciousness of love and acceptance of all people—something that we could have learned centuries ago from the native cultures, if only we hadn't perceived them as inferior.

Besides the traditional ones, there are also the spiritual and metaphysical grouping systems, which try to classify humans based on, for example, their birth attributes (astrology), their life energy, or their sacred animal association (Chinese and American Indian roots). Whatever you think of astrology and some of these other seemingly unscientific systems, they have been recognized and identified institutionally as some of the oldest sciences, having been found in many of the most ancient texts of human studies. All of these systems, ancient and current, exist to help humans better understand humans.

Nancy Ann Tappe authored a book in 1982 called *Understanding Your Life Through Color.*[2] This is the first known publication where the behavior patterns of these new children were identified. Nancy classified certain kinds of human behavior into color groups, and intuitively created a startlingly accurate and revealing system. Metaphysical in nature, the book is fun to read, and you can't help but identify your own traits somewhere in her system, laughing at yourself and marveling at how accurate it seems to be. Nancy continues to give lectures and workshops on human behavior throughout the world.

For those who think that classifying humans according to color groupings is weird and only for those interested in metaphysics, we would like to let you know about a brand new book called *The Color Code: A New Way to See Yourself, Your Relationships, and Life* by Hartman Taylor, Ph.D.[3] This book has nothing whatsoever to do with the Indigo Children. We only mention it here to show you that the association of colors with human attributes is not just for the spooky group! Hartman's book deals with the Hippocratic or medieval model for typing personalities—sanguine, melancholy, phlegmatic, and choleric—and assigns colors to them: red, blue, white, and yellow.

As we mentioned, Nancy Tappe's color groupings are intuitive, but are also very accurate, based on practical observation. One of the color groups in her work is—you guessed it—Indigo. This color classification reveals the new type of child very accurately . . . and did so 17 years ago! (At least someone was paying attention.) We think Nancy is owed kudos for her insight and awareness of human nature. If you are interested in such things as prophecy, chapter 3 will reveal a television personality who actually predicted the new "dark blue" children!

Jan did her research and found Nancy. She felt it was necessary to speak personally to Nancy for this book, and to interview her with some basic questions about what Nancy calls the "Indigo life color." We both felt that a good way to start the discussion of the Indigo phenomenon was to present what Nancy had to say, since she actually identified and introduced the whole thing. Jan's interview with Nancy continues throughout this book, with portions presented as the subject matter demands.

Introduction to the Indigos
Nancy Ann Tappe,
interviewed by Jan Tober (Part I)

Nancy, you were the first one to identify and write about the Indigo phenomenon in your book, Understanding Your Life through Color.[2] *What is an Indigo Child, and why do we call them Indigos?*

I call them Indigos because that's the color I "see."

What does that mean?

The life color. I look at people's life colors to learn what their mission is here on the Earth plane—what they're here to learn, what their syllabus is. Up until somewhere in the 1980s, I felt that there were going to be two more colors added to the system, because we had two disappear. We had the fuchsia disappear, and we had the magenta become obsolete. So I thought those two life colors would be replaced. I was shocked when I found one person who was fuchsia in Palm Springs, because it's a color that went out in the early 1900s, or so I was told.

I was telling everybody that there were going to be two more life colors, but I didn't know what they were going to be. While I was looking for these, I "saw" the Indigo. I was doing research at San Diego State University, trying to get a comprehensive psychological profile set up that could withstand academic criticism. At that time, a psychiatrist named Dr. McGreggor was working with me.

I'm trying to think of another doctor's name, but I can't remember it. He's at Children's Hospital, but he was the first one I really took note of, because his wife had a baby and she was not supposed to have children. The baby was born with a very bad heart murmur, and he called me to ask if I would come look at the boy and see what I "saw." So I went down and I looked, and that was when I really got established that this was a new color not in my life color system. The baby died about six weeks later—it was very quick. That was the first physical experience I had that showed me the children were different. That's when I started looking for them.

I quit teaching at San Diego State in 1975, so I know it was prior to that. I really didn't make a big issue out of it until 1980 when I started writing my book. It took me two years to get the book printed—1982 for the first edition, and then 1986 for the current edition. So it was somewhere in the '70s that I noticed it.

In the '80s, I really labeled it and started the personology process. Because then we had some kids that were five, six, and seven years old, and I could look at them and "read" their personality and see what it was about. The major thing I learned was that they did not have a syllabus as we do—they still don't. They won't have one for eight more years. At about 26, 27, you're going to see a big switch in the Indigo Children. The switch is going to be that their purpose will be here. The older ones will get really solid in what they're doing, and the younger ones will come in with a clearance on what they're going to do in life.

It sounds like it's still kind of up to us what is going to happen.

It's still in research. That's why I have delayed and delayed putting out any book on the Indigos. I'm glad you guys are doing it.

There seems to be a tremendous interest, a tremendous need to know.

Right. There is, because people don't understand these Indigos. They're computerized children, which means that they're going to be more head than heart. I think these children come in with some mental visualization rules down pat. They know that if they can label it, it's theirs. They are technologically oriented children, which tells me we are going to become even more technological than we are today. At 3 and 4, these kids understand computers that adults at 65 cannot understand.

They are technological children—children born for technology, which means that we can easily predict what we will see in the next ten years—technology that we didn't even dream of. I believe that these children are opening a gate, and that we are going to get to a point where nothing has to be labored over, except within our heads.

I agree with you.

That's their purpose. What I see is that in some cases environmental training has so blocked them that sometimes these children kill. Now I always believe in a paradox. We have to have the dark, and we have to have the light in order to have choice. Without choice, there is no growing. If we were just robots following something, then there would be no free will—there would be no choice—there would be nothing. I'm digressing, but I'm doing it for a reason.

The thing I've been telling my students lately is that if we are to believe in our beginnings, if we are to believe our Bible, it really says, "In the beginning there was a void, and darkness was upon the face of the deep." It always Was. And God said, "Let there be Light." He created good—He created light. He did not create darkness—it was always there. And then His whole process of creation was a maraud of separation. He separated the night from the day, the light from the dark, the earth from the heavens, the firmament from the air, the land from the waters. He separated woman and man and created male and female. The rule of creation is separation for choice; without a choice we are not growing.

So, what I see is that we've always had extremes, especially in this dimension. We've had the very extreme—the holiest of holies, and the most evil of evils. Most of us fit somewhere in the middle, aspiring to be holy while making mistakes. What I see now is that extreme becoming more integrated. The holiest of holies are becoming average people. The most evil of evils are becoming average people, and that balance is reaching a more refined level. These young children—every one of them I've seen thus far who kill their schoolmates or parents—have been Indigos. From what I've seen, only one of them was an Indigo humanist; the rest of them were Indigo conceptualists.

That's a very interesting observation—that all these children who are killing other children are Indigos. So what I am hearing you say is that their path is very clear, but somehow their mission got blocked, so their alternative is to get rid of what they think is blocking it?

That's a new form of survival. When you and I were children, we thought those horrible thoughts and we wanted to run away. But we were afraid. They're not afraid.

They're fearless, because they know who they are.

They believe in themselves.

Well, let's go into some of the other questions. To the best of your knowledge, when were the first Indigo Children noticed, and how prevalent is the overall percentage of Indigo births now?

My statement is that 90 percent of the children under ten are Indigos. I can't tell you when they first started coming in, but I know when I first started looking at it. My book *Understanding Your Life Through Color* was printed in 1986 so I know that I first started noticing it before then. I think I first started noticing it in 1982. I had noticed it long before then, but I didn't label it. But it took me until about 1985 to really see that they were here to stay.

Are there different types of Indigos? If so, what are they, and what are their characteristics?

There are four different types, and each of them has a purpose:

1. HUMANIST: First, there is the Indigo humanist, who is going to work with the masses. They are tomorrow's doctors, lawyers, teachers, salesmen, businessmen, and politicians. They will serve the masses, and they are hyperactive. They are extremely social. They'll talk to anyone, anytime— friendly, friendly, friendly. And they have very strong opinions. They're also awkward in their body, hyperactive as I said, and sometimes they will run into the wall because they forget to put on the brakes. They do not know how to play with one toy. Instead, they have to bring everything out— everything lays there—and they may or may not touch it. They are the ones who, if you tell them to go clean their rooms, you have to keep reminding because they get distracted. They go in their rooms, start cleaning, until they see a book. Then they sit down and read because they're ferocious readers.
    I was on a plane yesterday, and this one little Indigo—three years old—was fussing. His mother gave him the safety pamphlet, and he opened it up with all the pictures. He's sitting there, very seri-

ous, like he's reading it—very serious and intense with it. He studied it for five minutes, and I know he couldn't read, but he thought he was, I think. That's the Indigo humanist.

2. CONCEPTUAL: Then you have the Indigo conceptual. The conceptual Indigo is more into projects than people. They'll be tomorrow's engineers, architects, designers, astronauts, pilots, and military officers. They're not clumsy in their body, and they're often very athletic as children. They have control issues, and the person they try to control most is their mother, if they're boys. Girls try to control their fathers. If they get away with it, there's a big problem. This type of Indigo has tendencies toward addictions, especially drugs in their teenage years. Parents need to watch their behavioral patterns very closely, and when they start hiding or saying things such as "Don't go near my room," that's when their mother needs to search their room.

3. ARTIST: Then you have the Indigo artist. This Indigo is much more sensitive and oftentimes smaller in size, though not always. They're more into the arts. They are creative, and will be tomorrow's teachers and artists. Whatever they go into, they will be on the creative side of it. If they go into medicine, they may become surgeons or researchers. When they go into fine arts, they're the actor's actor. Between the ages of four and ten, they may pick up 15 different creative arts—do one for five minutes and put it down. So I always tell mothers of artists or musicians, "Don't buy the instruments—rent them!" The artist Indigo may work with five or six different instruments, then when they get to their teenage years, they'll pick one field or endeavor and become the artist in it.

4. INTERDIMENSIONAL: Then you have the fourth type, which is the Indigo interdimensional. They are larger than all other Indigos, and at one or two years of age, you can't tell them anything. They say, "I know that. I can do it. Leave me alone." They are the ones who will bring new philosophies and new religions into the world. They can be bullies because they're so much bigger and because they don't fit in like the other three types do.

Now, of all the physical life colors within the next 20 years, all will be gone except for red—and we're talking only about life color now. Only the mental colors—the tans, the yellows, and the greens; and the spiritual colors—the blue and violets—will be left. The Indigo humanist is replacing the yellow and the violet. The Indigo conceptual is replacing the tan, the green, and the violet. The Indigo artist is replacing the blue and violet. The Indigo interdimensional is replacing the violet. So obviously we have the violet in all four levels.

And they will be intuitive?

I have a story—it happened this morning. A friend has a grandson who is four years old. She had gone up to Santa Barbara to visit, and she took her daughter-in-law and Zachary, the little boy, out to dinner. The mother is constantly bragging about Zachary's school record and his swimming, and how his teacher in school was saying that he's a quick learner and does perfect back flips. He's absolutely fearless.

They went to a very nice restaurant and were going to have a big chocolate mousse dessert; the boy was looking forward to this. They brought out the dessert with this big fanfare and put it in the middle of the table and gave each of them a spoon to eat it with. His eyes got real big, and he laughed and reached out and pulled the dessert to his place setting and started eating. He's just sitting there eating, and finally the mother said, "Zachary, do you know what being fearless means?" He put his spoon down, furrowed his brow, and he looked at her and said, "Yes, I do."

"What do you think it means?" she asked.

He says, "I believe in myself!"

Four years old. That's what being fearless meant to him.

The statement that Zachary made is very clear. These children believe in themselves. If you're trying to tell them they're doing something wrong when they believe in themselves, they know that you don't know what you're talking about. So what I suggest to parents is that they set up boundaries where they don't tell their children *not to* do something.

Instead, say, "Now, why don't you explain to me *why* you want to do that. Let's sit down and talk about it. What do you think will happen? Just play it out with me. What do you think would happen if you did that?" When the child tells you what they think would happen to them, ask, "Okay, how would you handle that?" Then they'll tell you how they'd handle it.

You have to get an Indigo young one to do this, otherwise they won't participate—unless you've got a humanist, they're not going to talk to you about it.

By young, you mean, what age?

The minute they start talking, you talk openly to them. Get them to talk things through.

What about when they're babies?

You can do that when they're babies. You chat with them—you talk things through with them. Let them hear you chatter. "We're going to change your diaper now. We really need to do that so you don't get chafed, so you can be happy and I can be happy. You won't be crying, and I won't have to worry about it. And we'll all be happy, won't we? We're going to change your diaper."

You brought up another very important item: to treat these children as if they are adults when they begin to talk.

You cannot "talk down" to these children. They will spit in your eye if you talk down to them. They do not respect people based on their having gray hair or wrinkles. You have to earn your respect from the Indigos.

What haven't we covered here that you'd like readers to know about the Indigo subject?

I think I would say, "Just listen to them." Follow your gut level, and give up trying to be an authority. Let the children tell you what they need. Then tell them why you can't give it to them, or why it's okay for them to have it. And really, all it requires is listening. That's all. These Indigos are very open.

Again, being present.

That's right. You abuse these Indigo Children, and they'll go to school and tell the teacher, or they'll call the police—911. You've no doubt heard of many instances in the last few years of two- and three-year-old children saving their parents by calling 911, or things of that nature. If these kids are abused, they will go to an authority automatically. They will do that—and we get upset over that.

I like to call us the Rainbow Bridge from where we are to them.

I think that's true. I call them the bridge from the third dimension to the fourth dimension. The third dimension is a reasonable dimension—a *thinking* dimension. The fourth dimension is a *being* dimension. Here we talk about love and honor and peace and happiness and all of that, but we rarely ever practice it. We're getting better at it. In the fourth dimension, we will practice it. And we're beginning to realize that war is futile and that putting someone down is just another way of killing yourself. These children already know it.

The first Indigo workshop I did, we had the parents and the children there. They had baby-sitters come in and take care of the children, one baby-sitter for every four children. In the afternoon we brought the children in the room, and the parents could watch them interact and ask questions. We had an old electric typewriter, so we set it in the middle of the floor, and we had our other little things around. We didn't have a computer to set on the floor, but as I said, these kids are electronic children, so one child sat down at the typewriter, and all the other children were off playing. This was an amazing experiment.

So one would play with it, then another kid would come and sit down and watch. After a while, the one who was playing with the typewriter got up and left—and the next scooted over, and from somewhere in the crowd another came over and sat down and watched. And they went through that drill as if they were standing in line—but there was no line.

That's right, because these children don't queue up.

Right, and the parents watched that. Only one child out of about 15 went and sat on their parent's lap. The others paid no attention to their parents at all.

What year was this?

I think it was in 1984. These children . . . all they ask for is to be respected as children and to be treated as human beings—no differentiation between children or adults.

There's another funny story about my grandson. When he was eight, my daughter was one of these people who would not let him have weapons. He couldn't have guns and couldn't play with war things. She certainly didn't want him to have any electronics. When he was just about three, I was in my bathroom one morning curling my hair, and I have two curling irons, one cold and one hot. I was using the hot one, and he picks up the cold one and goes, "Bang-bang."

So I picked up mine and went, "Bang-bang." So we started running through the house, "Bang-bang-bang!" My daughter said, "Mother, you are not supposed to do that with him." I said, "He started it!" So we had great fun.

When he was eight, he came to me and he said, "Mano, you know what I want for Christmas?" I said, "No, what?" He said, "A Nintendo™ set!" My daughter, through clenched teeth, said, "Don't you dare." I laughed and thought, *You know, I'm his grandma and he asked me. She's just going to have to deal with it.* So as I was going out of town, I bought him a Nintendo set and left.

I came back two months later, and she called me and said, "Mom, I really want to thank you for giving Colin the Nintendo set." I said, "Oh sure, sure, I know." She said, "No, I'm serious. I really want to thank you, because I realized I couldn't take it away from him. I also realized that I had to be in charge, so I started 'selling' him Nintendo time. I told him that if he did his chores on time he would get so many minutes on the Nintendo. And he was getting all kinds of notes from school for noncooperation. So I told him, 'When you are cooperative at school, you'll get ten minutes on the Nintendo. When you have raised your grades up a level, you'll get so many minutes on the Nintendo. If they go down, you lose so many minutes on the Nintendo.'"

Well, he would come home from school, and he would do his chores and ask, "Do you have anything else you want me to do?" My daughter would say, "Well, you could do this." He would ask, "How many minutes on the Nintendo?" His math went from a D to an A. Two weeks after that, the teacher called and asked, "What happened to Colin? He is a different student." So Laura told her. She said, "For God's sake, keep it up. He's the best kid I've got now!" In school, the teacher said he'd come up to her and ask, "Is there anything I can do for you?" Before he went home, he'd go up to her and ask, "Can I do anything to help you?" She would tell him, then he'd go home and tell his mother what he did, and how much Nintendo time he expected for that. She gave it to him! He became an A student.

A lot of people talk about the Internet being bad for kids, and how there are dangerous things on it. But if parents have talked to their children and have been open with them, teaching them where to make choices, these kids do not get entrapped in that. It's the ones who need attention that get entrapped. These kids are smart. But they are like us—we make stupid choices sometimes out of need, and they do, too, if they're needy. But if we keep them settled, they make very wise choices.

They're great kids.

Is This Real?

Perhaps you are not interested in people who "see" colors. What follows next are reports and discussion from four Ph.D.'s and a schoolteacher regarding the subject of Indigos.

Do Nancy's classifications of Indigo types bear out in what the professionals are seeing? Dr. Barbra Dillenger thinks so.

Barbra Dillenger, Ph.D., spends most of her waking hours counseling. She is a specialist in human nature and concentrates on helping with the perception of an overview of life, reasons for living, and life lessons. She sees and embraces change and is aware of the many "types" of humans, and how such typology profoundly relates to helping them realize who they are. She has indeed seen the Indigo types and is not hesitant to give us this information. We applaud her marvelous contribution to this book.

About the Indigo Child
Barbra Dillenger, Ph.D.

As Nancy Tappe discovered in her observation of Indigo Children, there are four different types: the humanist, the conceptual, the artist, and the most rare type, the interdimensional. They all have similarities in their behavior, but there are also distinct differences. Here are three real-life experiences with Indigo Children: one with an artist, one with a humanist, and the last with a conceptual.

The Artist—A Story of Mission

Travis is an Indigo artist. He has been gifted with musical talent. At age four, he played his first public concert on the mandolin. He developed a young Indigo band at around age five, and after winning contests nationally at nine, they recorded their first CD. At 14, he had a top-ten hit off his solo album. All the songs were written, arranged, and played by him. He is considered to be, according to the music critic of the *Chicago Tribune*, the Mozart of the mandolin. The following incident happened at one of his concerts.

My husband and I had gone specifically to hear him perform in front of an audience of approximately 3,000 people. While in the ladies' room, I overheard two women conversing. One was saying, "My husband insisted that I come. He thought it would make me feel better." As I listened, I discovered she had just had a baby. She'd lost the child two weeks after birth and was still wearing maternity clothes. My heart swelled with grief.

In the meantime, Travis went on stage. During the performance, he played a song he had written at age nine, "Press On," about the death of his grandfather. This song happens to be one of my favorites, speaking to life's many experiences and how, with the help of God, we must press on. After a standing ovation, the concert was complete; my eyes fell on the same young woman I had seen in the rest room. She was talking with Travis. She said to him, with tears in her eyes, "That last song you sang has helped to heal me. Thank you. I'm so glad I came."

Travis thanked her; when she was out of sight, he turned to his guitar player and said in true teenage lingo, complete with a high five, "Right on—that's what it's all about." My heart again swelled, sending life through my body. He is still playing and composing at the ripe old age of 17. Truly an Indigo Star-baby on a mission.

The Humanist—A Story of Home Discipline

Todd is an Indigo humanist. While visiting his grandmother's home, an uncomfortable incident occurred. There was a beautiful musical clown doll with a china face sitting on Grandma's bed. It was her favorite doll, a gift from her husband. The clown's sad countenance reminded Todd of something in his "past"—so he found a way of smashing the doll's head into tiny pieces. He did this with great vigor. Grandma was visibly shocked. Todd was three or four and clearly without guilt. After regaining composure (she had already picked him up and set him on the couch), Grandma asked, her voice shaking, "What is your most important toy?"

"Police truck," said Todd.

Grandma said, "Can I come to your house now and smash your new police truck?"

"No," said the wide-eyed Todd.

"Well, this house is Grandpa's and mine, and we don't break things on purpose in this house." She continued, "We like our house to be a happy house, so if you were Grandma, what would you tell Todd to do right now?"

Todd thought over the situation and said, "I probably need a time-out." He went to another room of the house, isolated from a party in progress, closed the door, and sat all alone. In a few minutes, Grandma went into the room and talked with Todd about anger, fear, and positive expression (all in four-year-old language, of course). What we see here is the Indigo humanist (who loves people and freedom) choose a time-out for isolation, even at this young age. This self-imposed confinement was, to Todd, a fair exchange for his inappropriate behavior.

Grandma now has a beautiful new angel doll, a gift from a good friend, and this doll has a cloth face.

The Conceptual—A Story of School and the Need for Change

Tim is a young 12-year-old who came to my office with his frustrated mother. He would not go to school. He saw no value in the hours spent there. He particularly did not like his English class. (I think his mother's intention was for me to convince him to return to school!) Tim is an Indigo conceptual and very into the world of computers. I asked Tim, "Why do you not like English?"

He responded, "The teacher is stupid—she wants me to read Huck Finn." I suggested that he could indeed be smarter than some teachers, and pointed out that he could also still learn from them. I told him that English is a requirement in school, yet there are other ways to learn. And then I asked him how he was going to solve this situation. Tim immediately had an answer.

He told me that he and a few of his friends who felt the same way had started an English group after school. They were clearly not interested in Huck Finn. Instead, they were using the Internet. They were looking for a sponsor who would stay after hours and supervise them while still at school. I told him this was an excellent idea. Mother's mouth dropped open as I suggested that she support this solution and help him find a willing teacher.

Tim felt understood, and his body relaxed. I hear that while this has not solved all of Tim's school challenges, he has substituted his supervised Internet course for his other English class. Now he is once again going to school. His brilliant, conceptual idea shows the beginning of a change in our sometimes rigid, authoritarian school structure. So much of the current school structure does not serve the enlightened Indigo thinking. His mother, in the meantime, has become an active advocate of educational reform.

Smarter Than We Were?

Within the realm of the Indigo discussion, still another related phenomenon is occurring. All parents want to think that their child is smarter than the norm. What is being reported actually confirms this! So you are not crazy, Mom! The norm may have to be changed, however, so that it represents a new paradigm of measurement for children.

Do you feel that your child really is smarter than you were, or than other children you have raised in the past? Perhaps the "smarts" are being diagnosed as a problem, when the reality is that they should be seen as an asset. Could the "smarts" actually be causing dysfunction? How can you know? Are the schools unprepared for smarter kids? (You've had that intuitive thought all along, I'll bet.) Are Indigo Children generally smarter than most of us parents were as kids? For that matter, are most of the new children being born (Indigo or otherwise) coming in with new intelligence and wisdom?

This is a question that may begin to sound alarms all over the country. Noticed any news reports lately trumpeting that our kids are not being prepared well enough by our grade schools, and that nationally they are "testing" below average? Of course you have. However, all is not what it seems, and the following may give you pause for thought on this subject . . . as well as an indication that something is happening universally with our kids.

There is indeed evidence that today's children are far better equipped mentally than the schools are able to keep up with them—or, perhaps, to correctly diagnose the issue. Here is a quote from the cover of *The Rising Curve: Long-Term Gains in IQ & Related Measures.*[4]

> It is commonly lamented that children's educational abilities are declining rapidly and that schools are failing to prepare children for critical life tasks. Yet, psychometricians have discovered a curious trend that contradicts that dirge: IQ scores have in fact shown an astonishing rise over the last 50 years, and scores between white and minority students are converging. This trend, dubbed the "Flynn Effect" after James Flynn, the social scientist who first documented it, is the focus of this provocative book. . . . Is it possible to compare IQ scores from one generation to the next? Which environmental factors most affect IQ? What kind of intelligence do psychometric tests actually measure? Leading experts in nutrition, psychometric research, sociology, and cognitive, social, and developmental psychology debate the source of the Flynn Effect, along with the much-discussed dysgenic hypothesis, made popular by Charles Murray in *The Bell Curve.* A must-read for those who seek the latest scholarship on intelligence and its measure.

Let's discuss the attribute of IQ and "smartness" directly within the subject of the Indigo Child. We would like to introduce a wonderful contributor to this book, **Dr. Doreen Virtue.**[5] Besides her passion for children, she is a nationally renowned bestselling author (with *The Lightworker's Way* and *Divine Guidance*). She has been mentioned in several national magazines for her philosophy, and her in-depth studies are bringing scientific fact together with heretofore unsubstantiated metaphysical thought. She will be featured again in this book in chapters 2, 3, and 4.

Gifted or Troubled?
Doreen Virtue, Ph.D.

We know that Indigo Children are born wearing their God-given gifts on their sleeves. Many of them are natural-born philosophers who think about the meaning of life and how to save the planet. They are inherently gifted scientists, inventors, and artists. Yet our society, built upon the old energy, is smothering the gifts of the Indigo Children.

Many gifted children are mistakenly thought to be "learning disabled," according to The National Foundation for Gifted and Creative Children,[6] a nonprofit, nonsectarian organization, whose main objective is to reach out and help these precious children. According to leaders of this organization, "Many gifted children are being destroyed in the public educational system. Many gifted children are being falsely labeled with ADHD. And many parents are unaware that their child could be potentially gifted."

They list the following characteristics to help you identify whether your child is gifted:

- Has high sensitivity.
- Has excessive amounts of energy.
- Bores easily—may appear to have a short attention span.

- Requires emotionally stable and secure adults around him/her.

- Will resist authority if it's not democratically oriented.

- Has preferred ways of learning, particularly in reading and math.

- May become easily frustrated because they have big ideas but lack the resources or people to assist them in carrying these tasks to fruition.

- Learns from an exploratory level, resisting rote memory or just being a listener.

- Cannot sit still unless absorbed in something of their own interest.

- Is very compassionate; has many fears such as death and loss of loved ones.

- If they experience failure early, may give up and develop permanent learning blocks.

Sounds like a description of an Indigo Child to me—doesn't it to you? The organization concurs with our findings that "gifted children may also withdraw when they feel threatened or alienated and may sacrifice their creativity in order to 'belong.' Many children that we test exhibit a high IQ, but they often exhibit 'frozen' creativity as well."

Kathy McCloskey, Ph.D., is another of our scientific advisors in this book on the subject of the Indigo Children.With hands-on experience and case histories at hand, her contributions here are also greatly appreciated.

The New Powerful Children
Kathy McCloskey, Ph.D.

I have completed formal psychological testing over the last year at my community mental health center with three children who are clearly Indigo. All three children were referrals from a child psychologist at this site who was "mystified" by parents' and teachers' reports of the conduct and attentional problems these children exhibited. When in her office, they showed little or none of these symptoms, yet the other adults around these children adamantly reported they were "out of control" either at home, at school, or both.

Now the psychologist, whom I will call "Amanda," has a beautiful style of treating all her child clients with love and respect; she refused to take these reports at face value since they didn't match her own experience. She requested formal testing.

The first child referred was a 14-year-old Caucasian female. She had been taking her biological parents' car without permission (and without a driver's license) and leaving the house to hang out at the local 24-hour shopping center. She had been held back a year due to poor school performance, and was being ostracized by peers and teachers due to her advanced physical development and "wise-cracking" verbal style. Also, she would never let her parents "win" an argument. Her mom and dad reported that they were at their wit's end!

This child tested out with an IQ of 129 in her verbal abilities and 112 in her visual-spatial performance abilities (69 and below is deficient, 70–79 is borderline deficient, 80–89 is low average, 90–109 is average, 110–119 is high average, 120–129 is superior, and 130 and above is very superior). She tested within the superior verbal range for all language-based performance scores on a school-based knowledge test, and the lowest scores she obtained were "average" for her age and grade level!

In other words, she had no areas of weakness—in fact, she scored higher overall than others her age—in either her cognitive ability or her school-based knowledge, even though she'd been held back to repeat a school year! What was happening here?

This young woman had been put on Ritalin and Cylert, two of the "premier" drugs for ADHD, without success. Her parents reported that she had "always been this way" and that nothing they tried had "worked." When talking with her, it was obvious that she was interacting at a very wise, adult level; her face and eyes also revealed this. She seemed, in the vernacular, to be a "wise old soul." The problem was, no one but her was recognizing this!

Amanda, her new counselor, and I (through testing and clinical interviews) could see it clearly. This young woman, thanks to the apt intervention of her parents, is now enrolled in a special, individualized learning environment. This was not easy! Her parents had to apply for a scholarship to this very expensive but highly effective school. Yet she got in and is doing exceptionally well, since her parents were open to feedback, took it seriously, and now treat their daughter as the special, gifted Indigo Child she is.

The second child referred was a nine-year-old African-American male. He had been adopted three years earlier by his two African-American fathers who had recently moved here from out of town. Both fathers reported that their son was "hyperactive" since he could not sit still, was always moving, and had recent reports from teachers that he was disruptive in school (blurting out answers, bothering other students, getting out of his seat without permission, and so on). His dads were afraid that they were seeing the beginnings of a physical imbalance with their son, since he was the biological child of a drug addict.

They also wondered whether he could be experiencing the aftermath of unstable home and school situations during his early years, since he had been in and out of foster homes for most of his young life. Teachers were recommending ADHD medications, but his parents wanted to "find out for sure" what was happening before going down such a drastic path.

While this young man scored in the high average range in both his verbal and performance ability IQ measures (116 and 110, respectively) but below the gifted range, he had two subtests that were elevated into the very superior level: knowledge of social rules and norms, and abstract cognitive ability. His school-based performance measures showed he was performing in the superior range in all subject areas, suggesting he was an "overachiever."

My best guess, however, is that his school-based performance was a more accurate measure of his actual abilities than the IQ. This sometimes happens when truly gifted children have a chaotic or impoverished early environment, as was the case with this young man. It is highly probable that his two superior subtests from the IQ test were more representative of his actual potential and abilities.

In any case, once again, this child was being labeled as ADHD when in fact his actual performance was far above average. Also once again, the real problem was that no one at his school was recognizing this! Just as with the first child, it was obvious that he was interacting with others at a very intelligent, adult level, and his face and eyes projected this. He also seemed to be a "wise old soul."

Yet what could be done about all his extra physical energy? His parents were already providing clear structure at home, with rules and expectations spelled out (which the child himself had helped create). They gave him plenty of appropriate outlets for his physical energy and helped him "act out" certain lessons (by physically expressing things, repeating things out loud, rocking and standing on one leg while memorizing, acting out roles in stories, and so on). They agreed to take these "lessons" to his teachers—actually, we spent most of our time trying to figure out how they could best approach his teachers so that they would not get defensive or feel that they were being told how to teach.

The third and final referral was an eight-year-old African-American male who looked much younger than his age. He was living with his biological mom, stepfather, and 18-month-old half-brother. This young man was brought to Amanda by his mom because on two recent occasions he had been taken home by the police for walking away from school, trying to get home to his mom. He had also been telling his mom he wanted to die and would soon kill himself, and when asked what he planned to do, he would just shake his head and stare at the floor.

This young man, as well as his younger brother, really shook me up. In many ways, it was as if my previous two experiences with gifted Indigo Children were meant to prepare me for the children now sitting in my office. The eight-year-old calmly looked me in the eyes and told me that life wasn't worth living if his mom couldn't show that she loved him—he said he was sorry he was here! His younger brother had the same old face and eyes, and although relatively pre-verbal, he cocked his head and stared deeply into me. I swear on a stack of Bibles that this child was telling me, through his actions, not to reveal his secrets—whew!

Anyway, according to their mom, the older son routinely took care of the younger without being asked and seemed to know what to do without being told. However, she also reported that outside of this, he was a "terror." She said that since preschool, he had been physically "hyperactive," always talked back, always had to "have his way," and was very manipulative, as if he could tell how others wanted to be perceived and then would "play" on that. Two years ago, she had taken him to another therapist, but had stopped going when his behavior improved. Now, though, nothing could get him to behave, and she definitely wanted to start him on Ritalin.

His mom also said that her oldest child thought no one loved him, although she loved him dearly. She told me that caring for her youngest son took up all her time and that her husband didn't help at all with child care. On top of that, she said they had moved households and school districts at least once in each of the last four years due to her husband's employment. She also said that although she'd rather stay home with her children, economic necessity drove her to return to work. She said she wished her husband would take a more active role in both of her sons' lives, since she knew that her oldest missed his "real" dad, who had been in and out of prison over the last few years and had virtually no contact with him.

Neither Amanda nor I were prepared for the results of the testing. This eight-year-old tested in the extremely gifted range (IQ of 130 or above) across all ability levels, and only scored in the average range on the school-based testing when it came to writing performance (all other school-based testing areas were in the range of his very superior IQ). Even though his school learning had been disrupted over the last few years, his teachers and mom noted that he didn't "pay attention" at home or school, and he didn't fit the "ideal" student/son model, his cognitive and school performance scores were found only once in every 10,000 children his age!

I had a taste of what his parents and teachers dealt with when I first met him. He picked up and examined everything in my office, even opening drawers. My numerous requests that he take his seat were ignored. Therefore, I switched gears and addressed him in a calm, quiet, adult manner. I told him that it hurt my feelings to have someone come into my place and handle my things without permission. I told him that I felt as if he didn't like or respect me. I asked him if anyone had ever gotten into his things without asking, and he related two instances of this, one at home and one at school. He then apologized. I accepted his apology, and we shook hands as peers.

Throughout every interaction with him, spaced over four weeks of testing, he never again exhibited any behavior that was intrusive or that could be considered "inappropriate." He was attentive, polite, and worked hard during testing. Amanda had experienced a similar incident, handled it in the same way, and achieved the same results. The key word for this young man was *respect*! Once again, no one was recognizing him for who and what he was.

As of this writing, Amanda and I are still trying to figure out how to best present our findings to his parents, since we don't want to blame them for his "problems," and we know that his mom is coping with great pressure. Yet, only they can change his environment in order to help him learn how to deal with everyday limitations and expectations.

In summary, here are two main ways to identify Indigo Children:

1. If the Indigo Child has been identified as a "problem," testing is essential.

    • While not all Indigo Children will test in the "gifted" range across the board, most if not all will exhibit at least one area (or subtest of the IQ test) in the very superior range.

    • School-based performance, more often than not, will be at least in the average range.

2. If a child is believed to be ADHD, chances are they are Indigo!

    • Look for a range of "disruptive" behaviors that others mistake for ADHD.

    • Indigo Children will be labeled as hyperactive troublemakers who won't "listen," since the old ways, such as direct requests, will not work.

Working with Indigo Children is akin to working on ourselves. The lessons they teach are obvious! I've been an "official" psychologist interacting with these children, and have been delighted to use the "force of my expertise" to advocate for appropriate changes. However, we need more people like Amanda, who recognize that things are not always as they seem with these children.

I feel privileged to have helped Amanda with these three kids. I feel great respect for these new powerful children.

Teachers and Authors Speak

Most of the people we meet who deal with children are working in the trenches—they are schoolteachers, day-care workers, or teacher's aides. These men and women report to work every day with groups of today's kids. Often, they have had decades of experience with children and tell us how amazed they are at the changes they are seeing.

Parents, we all want to tell you that *there is hope!* Many professionals who are dealing with your children are extremely aware of the changes at hand. The "brick wall" you may hit with the educational system is the *system,* not necessarily the people in it. Many times they can't tell you that—yet as soon as you leave their office, their frustration probably surfaces. They have already heard what you are telling them, but have no work model for it and can't do anything about it.

In chapter 2, we will give you more information about what you can do at home regarding education. But now, we wish you to meet **Debra Hegerle,** a teacher's aide in California. She's one of those in the trenches. Listen to the wise words of this teacher. She doesn't *study* Indigos—instead, she lives with them on a daily basis. Like many of you, she has one at home as well.

Indigo Children
Debra Hegerle

I have a seven-year-old Indigo son. I've been working as a teacher's aide in his classrooms through preschool, kindergarten, and now first grade, and I've observed his interactions with Indigos and non-Indigos of all ages. It's been interesting! In fact, trying to put it all down in writing has been a challenge because the children do so many subtle things.

Indigos process their emotions differently than non-Indigos because they have high self-esteem and strong integrity. They can read you like an open book and quickly notice and neutralize any hidden agendas or attempts to manipulate them, however subtly. In fact, they can see your hidden agendas even if you can't! They have inherently strong determination to work things through for themselves and only want outside guidance if it's presented to them with respect and within a format of true choice. They prefer to work situations out for themselves.

They come in with their intentions and gifts easily identifiable from birth. They can suck up knowledge like a sponge, especially if they like or are drawn to a subject, which makes them very advanced in their areas of interest. Experiencing life helps them learn best, so they create the experiences they need to help them with their current problem or area where they need to grow. They respond best when treated like a respected adult.

Not only are they masters at intuitively picking up on hidden agendas or motives, but they are equally masterful at turning those agendas back onto the people using them, especially their parents. Psychological "button pushing" often causes them to be labeled as nonconformists. If they notice that there is a hidden motive behind your attempt to get them to do something, they will resist strongly and feel perfectly justified in doing so. From their point of view, if you're not doing your work in the relationship, they can challenge you on it.

When I called them good "button pushers," what I really meant is that they're working with us adults to help us recognize where we are holding and using old, subtle patterns to manipulate them, which used to work but will no longer. So if you are constantly getting resistance from an Indigo, check yourself first. They may be holding up a mirror for you or be asking you in a nonconformist way for help in finding new boundaries, fine-tuning their own skills or talents, or going to the next level of growth.

Indigos have innate healing abilities that are usually already active; however, they may not know that they are using them! The most spectacular thing I observed was how they formed groups, adjusting and spacing themselves, especially around another child who might have been sick or upset—sitting and blending their energy field with that child's. Most often, they paired up one on one, but sometimes they formed groups and sat in either a triangular or diamond-shaped pattern. It wasn't done in an obvious way, but very subtly. When finished, they were off to something else.

It was amazing. They just did it, but they didn't want to discuss it; in some cases, they weren't even consciously aware of what they were doing or why! It was so natural to them that if a child needed something from the Indigos, they just went and sat next to them for a while, not even necessarily talking, and then they separated.

Another interesting thing was that, off and on throughout the year, the Indigos went through periods of attracting and repelling each other, or periods of really needing each other's company and then of *not* needing it. I'm not totally clear on this, but it seems to coincide with individual personal development. The closeness and concern they had for each other was never lost during those periods of separation, but they wouldn't go back together, either, until all was right for them.

Now I'll give you one little story regarding my Indigo son. Let me give you the background: My husband and his family are Chinese Americans, and I am of German/Finnish heritage. My husband's family places great emphasis on education, and the siblings were brought up with a strong need to succeed. This still sometimes spills over onto their children, in the form of whose are better, smarter, and faster. My husband and I agree about not participating in all this competitiveness, but that doesn't stop it from happening around us. To top it off, consider that out of the five grandchildren, my son is the only boy—that is, the only *male heir*—and I think you'll get a pretty clear picture of the undercurrents.

We were at my in-laws' house on Christmas day, and my son, who was almost four years old at the time, was showing off his Millennium Falcon™ (a *Star Wars*™ toy that was meant for a six-year-old) that he had received from us that morning. It was the giant one that opens up, and inside were all kinds of little compartments, similarly but not identically shaped. He wasn't interested in that portion of the toy at that time. He was only interested in pretending to fly it and shoot the rockets—living out his fantasies. One of his uncles asked to play with it and proceeded to take all the little doors off of all the compartments. He handed them to my son in a pile and asked, "Can you put this back together?"

It was a setup! All the doors were the same color, and the differences in shape and size were very subtle. Oh, and the tone of voice he used—like butter wouldn't melt in his mouth. This uncle has three daughters and a whole lot of personal agendas, so his actions were not a total surprise, but . . . I absolutely love what happened next.

I started to intervene, and my son turned and looked me, dead in the eye, with a look on his face I'll never forget. He looked at me to see what I was going to do, and in the instant that it took for him to read my intentions, which were of Mommy Lioness—*I'm not going to let this happen to my son*—he responded just as quickly. He gave me a look that said, *Back off, Mom, I'm taking this one on myself*, and I felt the energy shift as he took command of the entire room. Everyone stopped talking and turned to look over at him. He calmly said to his uncle, "I don't know. I've never done that before; let me see." Then he proceeded to put that thing back together quickly and accurately!

When he was done, the energy shifted again, and he looked over at me as if to ask, "Was that okay?" I just smiled and said, "Good job." Everyone there caught the double meaning, including his uncle, who has never since done anything like that to my son or to anyone else's child in our presence.

No direct comments were made that night about the situation. We all just knew that we were each going to process it individually and privately, each getting our own lesson—all because this little one decided to learn for himself.

Indigos are born masters—each and every one! We have to understand that they fully expect every one of us to do what they are doing naturally, and if we don't, they keep pushing our buttons until we get it right—that is, until we become the masters of our own lives. So when my son did his thing, he taught everyone there a quiet lesson, including himself.

For me, the lesson was, *let him go; despite his age, he is capable. Stay aware and watch the process.* The process in this case was very interesting. He quickly and accurately sized up the situation, and determined his response based on what he wanted to experience. After making sure he had backup, he chose to confront the person directly, and at that point, he immediately called up all the energies necessary to complete the task. Afterward, he released it all back just as quickly and went back to his own business.

I've witnessed many similar situations that he or other Indigos handled in the same way. They will size up a situation and then choose their actions based on what they want to experience at the time. The only adjustments to this pattern that I've seen were based on what type of backup they had. In a safe environment, they have consistently used this pattern.

Safety is very important, because all children need to feel safe to fully explore their universe. For Indigos, safety means that it's okay to do things differently! Giving everyone this space is the best thing we can do for children and for ourselves.

Robert Gerard, Ph.D., is a lecturer, visionary, and healer. As a publisher, he owned and operated Oughten House Publications for many years. Robert is the author of *Lady from Atlantis*, *The Corporate Mule*, and *Handling Verbal Confrontation: Take the Fear Out of Facing Others.* He is currently touring and promoting his latest book, *DNA Healing Techniques: The How-To Book on DNA Expansion and Rejuvenation.* Robert offers workshops on DNA healing techniques, and is available for lectures and workshops worldwide.

Tired of hearing that the new kids are such a problem? Robert intuitively knew what type of child he had, and he had the wisdom to meet his challenge. Therefore, his Indigo Child was not a problem, but a joy! Jan and I find this to be a constant: Either the Indigos are bouncing off the walls with dysfunction, or they are the central joy of the family! It would not be fair if our work in this book did not reflect this.

Emissaries from Heaven
Robert Gerard

Fathering my seven-and-a-half-year-old daughter has been a blessing because she has manifested for me a multitude of subtle yet profound experiences. I consider each event a gift of life, an awakening. Many times I've been told that she was one of many Indigo Children sent to this planet. Speaking from a professional position, as well as a parent, I can truly say that Indigo Children are real and special. They need to be understood.

A loving parent with a gentle eye and an open heart readily sees that these children bear great gifts of awakenings and remembrances. These little ones keep us focused in the moment and remind us to play, laugh, and be free. They look into our eyes to let us see ourselves once again as we were in our own childhood. They seem to know what is happening in our lives and very keenly remind us of our spiritual whereabouts. As long as they remain uninhibited by parental powers and social distractions, they will step forward and say their piece.

My daughter, Samara Rose, has a knack for confronting us whenever my wife and I are not in a place of peace or harmony. As with many children born since the late 1980s, Samara (meaning "from God") came to this planet with a definite purpose, bringing forth intricate messages day after day. Indigos come to serve the planet, their parents, and their friends as emissaries from Heaven—bearers of wisdom, if listened to.

What does the term *Indigo Child* mean to me? The simplest answer may be that my daughter is an easy person to live with. After raising three other children who are all now adults, I can honestly say that Samara comes with a different tone and knowing. Indigo Children can be easy and loving; many of them look wise and have powerful eyes. They live profoundly in the now. They appear to stay happy, are very spirited, and have their own agenda. To me, the term

Indigo Children refers to special emissaries, sent from Heaven by the Father-Mother-Creator, bearing profound intent.

Indigo Children bring subtle messages that are beyond all our knowing. Take a good look at the children, listen to their message, and go within. This is how they assist us in finding our truth, our purpose, and our peace. *Look into their eyes.* Blessed are our Indigo Children. They know exactly what they came to this planet to accomplish. I stand firmly in support of this phenomenon—not just as a parent, but as a counselor—and I truly appreciate having this insight.

As a publisher, my home has often resembled a bed-and-breakfast, and every author, artist, and associate that has come over has invariably found themselves entertained by Samara. Up into her room they would go, to play and talk about who knows what. When they came down, they appeared to be more peaceful and cheerful. By the time I wanted to talk business, they were usually tired! She's made a mark on each—afterward, they always ask for her. The pattern becomes clearer each time: When she interacts with adults, she brings out their inner child and simplicity of being. On the other hand, she's a bit tough on her peers and finds herself being rejected or overadmired. I often have to coach her on expressing herself in a loving way.

Most Indigos see angels and other beings in the etheric. Time after time, they describe what they see in detail. This is not imagination—it's explanation. Among themselves, Indigo Children talk openly about what they see, until discouraged by others. Fortunately, more and more people are opening up and listening to these emissaries. Our fantasies about children are being replaced with curiosity and trust.

Indigos are fascinated with accuracy and how people interrelate. They are easily disturbed when things, especially conversation, are out of synchronization. They enjoy being spontaneous and get easily excited for no obvious reason. Many people have difficulty relating to these emissaries because they approach with built-in beliefs and rules that the children do not share.

When you were a child, how many times did you hear this infamous question: "What do you want to be when you grow up"? Instantly, you projected into a future occupation or activity. Didn't that take you out of the now? Asking "What do you want to be?" is a violation, a breakdown, an interference of being and staying in the moment. Children *are* all they need to be; they are themselves. Let's leave them alone so that they can be exactly who they are.

Problems the Indigos May Experience

I've explored some of the positive attributes of the Indigo Child, but here are three complications that I've witnessed, professionally as well as privately, with Indigo Children.

1. They demand more attention and feel that life is too precious to let it fly by. They want things to happen and often force a situation to meet their expectations. Parents easily fall into the trap of "doing" for the child instead of role-modeling or sharing. Once this happens, you can bet on the child following you around as if a string were attached.

2. These emissaries can become emotionally upset by peers who do not understand the Indigo phenomenon. They can't figure out why the others operate in anything but love. However, they are extremely resilient and able to help children in need, though this help is often rejected. When young, they may have trouble adjusting to these other children.

3. Indigo Children are often labeled as having ADD or some form of hyperactivity. Certainly many valid cases have been identified, based on chemical and genetic causes. But what about those cases that are misunderstood because science cannot accept

as therapeutically significant the child's occupation in the spiritual and etheric realms?

I have talked to children and adults alike who appear to be "hyper" or claim to have ADD, but in whom I see thought patterns that focus on the etheric and spiritual realms. These Indigos labeled with ADD cannot consistently relate to the linear mind or linear objectives. This is not a deficit, but a valuable characteristic. Providing a creative dialogue with these children, and permitting them to safely express their activities and orientation in the spiritual or creative realm, may be key in dealing with ADD.

Labeling oneself as hyper or having ADD can be more of a disservice to the individual than the symptom itself. It can easily lead the person to deny their inner mastery and to underestimate their abilities. Careful attention needs to be taken before one is labeled as, and begins treatment for, something that was not thoroughly investigated.

Will a subsequent generation of Indigo Children arrive on this planet? As parents and adults, do we appreciate the emissaries that the Father-Mother-Creator has sent? Are we prepared to *listen?*

We cannot doubt that they have arrived with a consciousness more equipped to handle the reality we all share. Let each of us remain pure in heart and open in Spirit, and accept these hand-delivered gifts of the emissaries from Heaven.

Warm and Fuzzy Stories about the Indigos

We would like to conclude this chapter with a couple more stories about Indigo Children. It only seems fitting, since every Indigo is so unique, so special. The best way to learn about Indigos is to meet them!

I wanted to share something wonderful that Emma did before she even knew how to walk or talk. . . . It's my family's little miracle.

In March of 1996, my father, who had been diagnosed with congestive heart failure, was at home surrounded by his loved ones, but fading fast. Too weak to eat, he slept in his chair most of the time.

Little Emma was only 15 months old. She could not utter any words, nor could she walk or stand—yet great understanding and compassion were already hers. Something was going on in that little brain of hers; somehow she knew that her grandpa didn't feel good and needed cheering up. So she crawled over to him, pulled herself to a standing position using his knees for support, and handed him her favorite stuffed bunny. It was incredible how that man literally sprang back to life, smiling and talking to her. This happened only two days before he passed away . . . our own little miracle! The photos we took are a great comfort.

— Jean Flores, Brooklyn, New York

My daughter was born in 1988. She was totally verbal and communicating perfectly by age two. At age three, one day at the playground, she went over to play with some older girls—who pretty much laughed in her face, believing she was much too young to play with them. Unfazed, my daughter came back to me and reported in a matter-of-fact way, "Mommy, they just don't know who I am!"

— Linda Etheridge, teacher

chapter two

What Can You Do?

A s you read the opinions in this chapter, we want you to remember that these contributors don't know each other—yet you are going to see a consensus of opinion as if they did! We know that when similar answers are collected independently, it usually reflects a common human experience—yielding *valid solutions!*

We are going to discuss what to do with Indigo Children from a behavioral and parenting perspective. Although the experiences and advice vary a bit, you are going to find tremendous similarities. Before we do that, however, we would like to share something that, in all fairness, you should know.

This entire chapter is filled with good advice and practical experience from experts, teachers, and parents who offer solutions to today's alleged new child-rearing puzzle. However, in spite of this, there are people telling us that we should just skip this entire section—perhaps this entire book! They are telling us that there is actually nothing we can do as parents to change our kids!

For example, an article titled "The Power of Their Peers" appeared in the August 24, 1998, edition of *Time* magazine.[7] In it, columnist Robert Wright comments on *The Nurture Assumption,*[8] by Judith Rich Harris, who argues that parents have little influence on their kids! Here are some quotations from Mr. Wright's article:

> Psychologists can call off their century-long search for the key to rearing a good child—not because they've found it but because it doesn't exist. . . . Judith Rich Harris states baldly that parents do not have "any important long-term effects on the development of their child's personality."

Evidently Ms. Harris believes that pivotal environmental influences outside the home shape a child's life, along with genetics. The children absorb values from outside, then combine them with a predisposition of inherited personality. This is what eventually shapes their lives, she reports, while the parents kind of "go along for the ride," helplessly watching.

Naturally we disagree with this theory, but we are publishing it so that *you* can be the judge. Please read her book if you wish, and when you are finished, see if this information resounds with your parental instinct, or with our material. Here is what Mr. Wright had to say in summary:

> Harris' core, convincing message—that man parents wildly overestimate their influence—may usefully calm some nerves in this age of high-anxiety parenting. But it may also do the opposite. These days much parental fretting is already going into the shaping of peer groups and their context. Which private school? Soccer on Saturday or French lessons? Birthday party at Marva Tots or the Discovery Zone? Relax. Science hasn't answered these questions either.

Naturally we believe that you *can* make a difference—a big one. We invite you to read this chapter with the knowledge that these contributors are experienced and have found the following suggestions to be solutions.

First, here is our own list of ten basics—what we have learned and experienced during our travels:

1. Treat Indigos with respect. Honor their existence in the family.

2. Help them create their own disciplinary solutions.

3. Give them choices about *everything!*

4. Never belittle them—*ever!*

5. Always explain *why* you give them instructions. Listen to this explanation yourself. Does it sound stupid—as in "because I said so"? If so, then revisit the instructions and change them. They will respect you for this and wait. But if you give them authoritative, dictatorial orders without good, solid reasons, these kids will take you apart. They won't obey, and what's more, they will give you a laundry list of why it is no good! Sometimes your reasons can be as simple as "because it will help me today—I'm really tired." Honesty will win as never before. They will think about it, then do it.

6. Make them your *partners* in raising them. Think about this aspect a lot!

7. As infants, explain to them everything that you are doing. They won't understand you, but your consciousness and honoring of them *will* be felt. It's a tremendous setup for when they begin to talk.

8. If serious problems develop, get them tested before you drug them.

9. Provide safety in your support. Avoid negative criticism. Always let them know that you support them in their endeavors. They will often rise to meet your verbalizations—and shock you in the process. Then, celebrate together! Don't *make* them achieve, but *let* them do it with encouragement.

10. Don't tell them who they are now, or who they are going to be later. They know better. Let *them* decide what they are interested in. Don't force them into a family craft or business solely because that's what the family has done for generations. This child absolutely won't be a follower.

We have a favorite story: While on a lecture tour, I found myself in the home of a family with a three-year-old Indigo Child. You could look into his eyes and see what an old soul he was. His parents knew who he was and were very successful in the task of getting him to interface in a meaningful way with the family. At dinner, instead of being told to sit down, he was asked to choose where to sit—the parents had thoughtfully prepared a couple of options. Therefore, a potential uncaring command became a loving request to choose. In both cases, the overview was that dinner was being served, and an expected action was required. The child looked at the situation, and you could actually see that he was taking responsibility for deciding which chair to sit on. The idea of rejecting "coming to dinner" was never there.

I also saw the child object once or twice later in the evening when he was tired and crabby, as all children get. He was firmly and appropriately disciplined with stern words and an accompanying action. He was treated correctly and with respect, but he still tried to push himself past his appropriate place, as all children do to test their power. Then came the expected disciplinary action, with a logical, calm explanation. The difference here was not in the way the child was disciplined, as much as in the way he was treated up to and during the problem. Throughout all of this, the child gets the point: "We treat you with respect, and you do the same with us."

Again, let's hear from the creator of the term *Indigo Children*: **Nancy Tappe.**

Being a Guide
Nancy Ann Tappe,
interviewed by Jan Tober (Part II)

Nancy, what is your advice to the parents of Indigo Children?

Just chat with them. Work them through their events instead of saying, "The answer is no!" These children will not accept that as an answer. If you say, "No, you can't ask questions," that kid will go out and find out by themselves. They will feel that you don't have the answers.

What about giving them choices at this point?

You must give them choices. However, you must walk them through it first. You say, "When I was your age, I did this, and this happened. How would you handle that?" And what they'll often do is to come right around to your process. My daughter did this dozens of times with her son, Colin. You can sit down with them and say, "You know, I've got a heavy day today, and I really need your cooperation because I'm going to be a little frazzled. So if you start pushing me, I'm going to scream. You don't like me screaming, and I don't like to scream. So here's the deal: You cooperate—you help me—and when we get done, we'll go have an ice cream cone." Then you'd better remember what you promised them!

You know, what you're saying is very interesting, because that sounds to me like really good advice even for husbands, wives, or friends.

Yes, absolutely. But you see, we have refined our communication skills. We had to learn them. These children are born with them.

So they're going to help us hone ours?

You betcha, and they're going to make us be honest about it. They really have massive personal power—that's just the way Indigos are. Sometimes it's better to let them have control.

If you isolate them, they will draw on your walls. They will rip the carpet off the floor. They will do destructive things if you isolate them from the crowd. If you are having a party and you put them to bed early, you will not have a quiet party—they will make sure everybody knows they're in the house. You cannot isolate the Indigo and get them to cooperate.

These children are demanding that we really practice family living, not just idealize it. They are saying, "I'm a member of the family, and I want a vote."

They're making us walk our talk.

Giving orders is not effective. This is where the school system is failing, because the school system has absolute rules without deviation—"don't ask, don't tell." These kids ask and tell. They ask, "Why? Why do I have to do that?" Or,

"If I have to do it, I'll do it my way." These children have the rules of our idealized world, not our real world, and they really expect us to be parents. They expect us to sit down and share quality time with them. We think that whatever we can afford is quality. They have a different opinion. They want us present, and they don't expect to do things just for the heck of it, either. They want some kind of tangible reward.

Just like adults do. Also, parents should remember this: If you are going to be with them—be with them! Be present in your body because they know the difference.

Or else tell them: "I'm going to flake out for a while." The kid will say, "Okay, I'll have ice cream while you're gone." The children don't care as long as the parents are honest. That's all they ask. Most of the time the Indigos are very cooperative on that level, unless you push them—then they stand their ground. They believe in themselves.

What is your advice to schoolteachers who must work with Indigo Children and non-Indigo Children together?

That has been a major issue. It is becoming less and less an issue because there are more and more Indigos.

Do you know of any school systems that really do work with Indigo Children?

The one that comes closest to it, especially here in the States, is the Waldorf System, which is a version of the Rudolph Steiner School; during World War II, Steiner moved his work out of Germany and set up his system in Switzerland.

[Note: see our information later in this chapter regarding alternate school systems.]

What type of therapy would you advise for a dysfunctional Indigo Child?

A good child psychologist. Unfortunately, a lot of psychologists are not trained to handle Indigos because they're trained in basic child psychology as set up by Spock, Freud, and Jung. None of that works with these children—well, some of it does, but not as well because these children are different. They are totally different.

I think the best psychologist for a Conceptual [see chapter 1] is a sports psychologist, especially for boys; for a Humanist or an Artist, go to an ordinary psychologist. An Interdimensional needs more staunch rules because they're very abstract; they need more ministerial counseling. Isn't that interesting?

Our counselors have to go through a major change in order to help these children, which is happening. In the past, in many ways, an esoteric psychologist was better because they would use their sensory system or their psyche or other alternative modes that the average psychologist was not permitted to touch. But that is changing fast, and today a lot of trained psychologists are using every metaphysical tool there is. This is really quite nice, and we are having a lot of doctors come out and use the alternative modes.

Let's again hear from our Ph.D. team, which knows quite a bit about the practice of child psychology, as they give advice to parents and teachers: Here is **Dr. Doreen Virtue**, and following her, **Dr. Kathy McCloskey**.

Parenting an Indigo Child
Doreen Virtue, Ph.D.

At my workshops and in my private practice, I'm often asked for help from loving parents who are frustrated with their children. "He just won't do his homework!" and "My daughter won't listen to a word I say!" are among the exasperated comments I hear. I'm the first to admit, both as a parent and as a psychotherapist, that raising an Indigo Child isn't the easiest activity—unless, that is, you shift your entire thought structure regarding the situation.

It doesn't take a psychologist or a psychic to point out this obvious fact: We learned many of our parenting behaviors from our own parents, the media, or even parenting classes. Unfortunately, these sources are all products of the old energy. They don't work in situations involving the new energy. And remember: Indigo Children are 100 percent new energy.

Our task as parents is to shelter our Indigo Children from remnants of the old energy, and help them to always remember their Divine origin and mission. We can't afford to have these Indigo Children incur mass amnesia about their purposes—the world depends on them!

Therefore, the first step is to be flexible in our viewpoints and expectations regarding our children. After all, why is it so important for us that our children do well in school? Now, I am not suggesting in any way that education is unimportant, but let's be honest: Why do you get upset when your child's teacher calls with a negative report? Does it recall your own childhood days when you were in trouble? If so, you aren't really angry at your child; you are afraid *on behalf of* your child.

On the other hand, maybe you believe that your child needs a "good education" to "make it" in the world. I would question this premise, as the new world before us rests on entirely different ideals. In the new world, a person's integrity (which can be determined telepathically, since we will all regain our natural psychic abilities within a few short years) will be the most important asset on a résumé. Education without integrity will be considered worthless by employers of the future.

By shifting our viewpoints and expectations about our child's behavior, we can approach parenting from a peaceful point of view. Admittedly, this can feel a little unsafe or threatening. As parents, our instincts tell us to protect our children. So, we automatically fight for our child's right to success, and this can often mean having fights with your child while you push him or her to do homework.

This is one of the first generations of parents of Indigo Children, so mistakes are bound to be made. Yet your soul and your child's soul agreed to incarnate together during this great time of the millennium shift. So at the soul level, you knew what you were in for when you signed a spiritual contract to parent an Indigo Child. Forgive yourself for taking on this difficult assignment, and know that God never gives us missions for which we are unprepared to succeed.

Let's read on and learn a few pointers from our next expert as she gives specific tips on how to respond to the seeming problems of parenting an Indigo. **Dr. Kathy McCloskey** was introduced in the last chapter.

Things to Remember When Raising Indigo Children
Kathy McCloskey, Ph.D.

1. Be creative when setting limits.
    *   Allow for extra physical energy. Incorporate this

into most situations (such as teaching, enforcing boundaries, and getting chores done).

- Allow the child's strengths to drive the limits, not the other way around. You may be surprised by what an Indigo can do. Test the limits in a safe way!
- Above all, ask the child to help determine the limits. In fact, many Indigos will be glad to set the limits themselves, with an adult's help.

2. Without giving these children adult responsibilities, treat them as adults and peers.

- Give these children adult explanations, a say in making decisions of all types, and above all, lots of choices!
- Do *not* talk down to them.
- Listen to them! They are wise, and will know things you do not.
- Respect them in all ways, as you would your own parents or a close, cherished friend.

3. If you say you love them, but treat them in a disrespectful way, they will not trust you.

- They will not believe you love them if you do not treat them in a loving way. All the words in the world will fall on deaf ears.
- The way you conduct your own life and "run" your own family is direct evidence to the Indigo Child about whether you are loving or not!

4. Interacting with Indigo Children is both work and a privilege.

- They will catch you in all deceptions. Don't even try it!

- When in doubt, ask not only the children them-selves, but also other adults with Indigo Children experience.

- Don't forget to take time to observe Indigo Children interacting with each other—there is *much* to learn here.

Don't forget: They not only know who *they* are, they also know who *you* are. You cannot mistake the look of an Indigo Child's eyes and face—very old, deep, and wise. Their eyes are the window to their feelings and soul. They can't seem to "hide" like others can. When you hurt them, they will be disappointed in you, and may even question the wisdom of "choosing" you! But when you love them and recognize who they are, they will open to you like no other.

Next, **Debra Hegerle** will recommend some books. Remember, most of the books mentioned in the text of this book are again found in the notes in the back.

Boredom and Honesty
Debra Hegerle

Indigos are open and honest—this is not a vulnerabili-ty, but their greatest strength. If you are not open and hon-est with them, they will still be so with you; however, they will not respect you. That's a serious issue with Indigos, because they will stand in their integrity with you, match-ing you push for push, until you either wake up to the real issue, back down, or give up. Of the three responses, giving up is the worst. They do not respect those who won't work through the process, and giving up means you're not doing your work. Backing down is okay because it shows them that you are still working on the issue, and they respect that. If you recognize the true value of this wonderful gift, then things turn out well because they don't expect perfection from you—but they do expect honesty!

Boredom can bring out arrogance in Indigos, so don't let them get bored. If they act arrogant, it means that they need a new challenge and new boundaries. Feeding their brains and getting them occupied is the best way to keep them out of mischief. However, if you do all this and they still get into occasional mischief, it's because they are creating a life experience for themselves that, if looked at closely, will reveal much about their life plan. Just flowing with it during those times works out best for everyone. You can distinguish this situation from boredom because either you won't be able to deter them, or you'll find out after the fact!

All parents, particularly parents of Indigos, could benefit greatly from the following books:

- *Back in Control—How to Get Your Children to Behave*, by Gregory Bodenhamer,[9] is based on the premise that you discipline your child from a position of respecting yourself and your child by giving them clear choices and clear consequences—and then, the most important part, following through.

- *The Life You Were Born to Live—A Guide to Finding Your Life Purpose*, by Dan Millman,[10] is an excellent guide to identifying and recognizing others' strengths and weaknesses and guiding them to manifest the most positive uses. (Works well for us, too!) Include your child in the process of understanding why they have their particular issues, challenges, and talents.

Indigos excel in an environment where boundaries are clearly set about what's not acceptable, but where open exploration within those boundaries is encouraged. This means that parents, teachers, and caregivers have to be able to set and keep clear boundaries, yet be flexible enough to change and adjust those boundaries when needed based on emotional/mental growth—and Indigos grow fast! Being firm but fair is necessary for their sake as well as our own.

Next, how about some real down-to-earth "do's and don'ts" for parents? The items in the following lists may sound very familiar—you may have heard them all your life, often from your own parents! A new paradigm for treating children has emerged that, although packed with common sense, is not always practiced. Do you find yourself echoing your parent's words to you when you speak to your children? Do you know what the energy of your actions and words communicate to these new kids with their "Indigo antennae" pointed at you?

Professor Emerita **Judith Spitler McKee** is a developmental psychologist, consultant, and early childhood educator. She is the author of 12 textbooks on children's learning, development, play, and creativity. She conducts workshops for parents, teachers, librarians, therapists, and medical practitioners.

Sending Potent, Positive Messages to Children
Judith Spitler McKee, Ed.D.

All children require personal and intense care, attention, time, encouragement, and guidance from adults. The overall tone of the adult-child interactions needs to be emotionally caring, loving, and soothing, as well as intellectually clear and stimulating. The verbal and nonverbal messages sent need to be consistently lighthearted and welcoming to children, as if they were invited and cherished guests in our lives.

Many times adults feel, act, and talk in ways that make children feel they are anything but welcome; rather, that they are actually bad, a burden, or a nuisance. These unwelcoming, heavyhearted messages are extremely damaging to the growth, learning, striving, and creativity of children who look to adults as models and for support. Children experience these messages as: *I'm a bad child, unwanted here.* These painful messages of fear lessen children's ability to respond and can seriously stunt their overall development.

Conversely, a stream of lighthearted, welcoming messages of growth is interpreted as: *I'm a good child; my world is positive and loving.* This view develops children's trust and opens up internal motivation to grow, learn, strive, and create.

Developing Trust or Mistrust with Children

Children develop trust as they learn in their bodies and spirits that their basic physical, emotional, intellectual, and creative needs will be met by the caregivers and special adults in their young lives. The messages sent and care given by adults must be more pleasant than painful, and more love-based than fear-based. From trust, a tapestry is woven of mutuality, connectedness, and respect between adults and children.

In the following situations, I will give examples of messages that are heavyhearted and unwelcoming in tone, as well as lighthearted and welcoming alternatives. The details can be changed for different ages or situations, but the consistency of the underlying message is what is most important in the interaction. The following are moments where you can make a difference:

1. Your child rushes in the back door covered in mud and weeping. She wants to be held, to take refuge from an upset in her world.

    Heavy/Unwelcoming: "Don't touch me with those dirty hands. You're a mess. Stay away from me!"

    Light/Welcoming: "When you wanted me to pick you up, I was thinking about my clothes getting dirty. You mean more to me than my clothes. Let's wash up. Would you like to find your favorite book, and we can snuggle together on the couch?"

2. Your child approaches you in the middle of a hectic moment in your life.

    Heavy/Unwelcoming: Your eyes roll as the child nears, and you think, *Here comes trouble,* or *Here he is again. Oh no, more work for me.* You assume a defensive body posture with shoulders erect and lips tightly sealed, as if steeling yourself for combat.

    Light/Welcoming: You put your hand gently over your heart, and think of the love you and your child each need and can share. Let your eyes soften and your body relax; now you can send that clear, loving message: You are welcome in my life.

3. Your children ask constant questions or need instructions or rules repeated often.

    Heavy/Unwelcoming: Abrupt, disinterested, annoyed, or sharp voice tones convey messages such as, *You really bother me! Go elsewhere,* or *You are unwanted here.* Consistently used, they can make the child feel unlovable.

Light/Welcoming: Think of your voice as a teaching tool, and practice modulating its tone and pitch. When you are very stressed or angry, take two deep belly breaths to bring revitalizing oxygen into your bodily systems so you can think more clearly. Then practice speaking more softly and at a slower speed.

4. Your children are out in the world, beyond your control.

Heavy/Unwelcoming: "Don't go on that slide! You could break your neck like that girl on the TV. Get down before you end up in the hospital." Or, "Don't talk to any strangers. Dangerous characters are lurking everywhere. Call me the second you arrive." Continually expecting the "worst" to happen fills your children with fear, a generalized uneasiness, or an actual physical readiness for danger. These negative emotions flood the body with specialized hormones for fear, fight, and flight that can greatly weaken the immune system, producing illnesses such as earaches or digestive upsets.

Light/Welcoming: "I know we've talked about safety and being careful with people you don't know. Do you want to ask me anything before you go to the concert with your friends? I know you'll be okay today because you are careful and know how to take care of yourself. I know you use your head and heart together. Remember, you can always call home if you need to or if you just want to talk. Okay?" Affirmatively stating the actions you desire will reinforce those habits in your child.

5. You broke a promise to your child.

Heavy/Unwelcoming: "Quit whining because we didn't go to the fair with your cousins. You'll get over it. Nobody took me places when I was your age." Here, you have neglected to discuss the reasons—no matter what they were—that you broke your promise. This would send the message that adults don't really care, or they can't be trusted to follow through.

Light/Welcoming: "I was so busy with other work that I completely forgot about taking you to the fair with your cousins. I'm sorry. Let's talk about our feelings."

Using Shame or Guilt with Children

Adults sometimes use techniques of shaming and inducing guilt because that is what they remember from their own childhoods. Also, these highly injurious techniques *seem* to work because children do act differently when shamed, especially if it is done in public. Actually, these techniques do *work*, but at a major cost to the child's developing personality! Shame and unnecessary guilt negatively affect the child's quest for individual expression. Shame and guilt are such powerful and painful emotions that they often block curiosity, play, and creativity. Children quickly learn not to be open or honest with others. Instead of relying on shame and guilt, think about and model the desired behavior, present encouragement to try again, explain consequences, and offer reasonable choices to children.

The following situations will show you how to overcome using shame tactics:

1. Your young or disabled child has had a toilet accident:

    Heavy/Unwelcoming: "Bad, bad, bad girl! You know better than to go in your pants (or on Grandma's new couch). You did that on purpose. Well, you can wipe up yourself and that smelly mess without me. Don't you ever do that again. Don't you embarrass me like that!"

    Light/Welcoming: "Uh-oh! Looks like you had an accident and wet your pants. That's okay. I'll help you put on clean clothes so you feel better." You can follow this up by reading and laughing together with Taro Gomi's book, *Everyone Poops*.[11]

2. Your child is dawdling, eating slowly, or refusing to eat certain foods.

    Heavy/Unwelcoming: "Hurry up! You're just being stubborn again and making me wait. Eat all your peas right now! If you won't eat the curried meatballs, you can stay in your chair all by yourself. I'm leaving, and when I get back, those meatballs better be gone, too. Don't be so fussy! If you don't eat all your food, you'll get sick."

    Light/Welcoming: "I want you to do what I do. I'm going to taste one spoonful of Aunt Jo's special beans and rice casserole." (Adult samples food without making a fuss.) "This is a little different from what we usually eat, but it's an interesting taste. Okay, now you taste one spoonful. Do you think Teddy Bear would like a taste with us?" Follow up by reading together, enjoying the book *This Is The Way We Eat Our Lunch*[12] or *Everybody Cooks Rice*.[13]

3. Your child is refusing to eat certain foods, either because of personal preferences, allergies, illness, fear of gaining weight and being unloved, or imitation of picky or dieting adults.

   Heavy/Unwelcoming: "I'm not waiting a second longer while you keep looking for no-fat, no-calorie food so you won't gain weight. Everybody's staring at us. You're acting like a child."

   Light/Welcoming: "Let's plan some menus together so we can find foods we want to eat. Here are two menus I would like. Here's an interesting article on what nutrients our bodies need and what foods provide them. Can we discuss it later?"

4. Your child has an obsessive, irrational, or exaggerated fear about a situation, person, or animal.

   Heavy/Unwelcoming: "For goodness' sake! It's only a seven-line verse you have to say at the District Assembly. Other kids have bigger parts than you do. You're acting like a real baby. Just go in your room, buckle down, and make me proud of you."

   Light/Welcoming: "Could you show me the verse you're going to say at the school assembly next week? I wonder if the teacher chose you because he knew you would do it well. Would you like to practice the verse by yourself, or do you want some coaching?"

5. Your child seems defiant of rules and adult authority, or hits your "hot buttons." At school, your child has told lies or cheated on assignments or other activities.

Heavy/Unwelcoming: "You miserable liar! You deliberately embarrassed me by telling that horrendous lie to your teacher (or cheating on the assignment, or missing dance or soccer practice). Well, one day when you really need help, don't expect it from me—or your teacher! You're grounded for four weeks! You don't deserve a chance to be heard after the awful lie you told—no remarks. Get out of my sight!"

Light/Welcoming: "I am very upset that you seem to have told a lie. I understand some of the situation from talking to your teacher, but I want to know more from you. We need to talk now about what happened and what you were feeling. Then we need to talk about how we can work this out. I need to be able to trust you to do what's right and honest in other situations. I need your cooperation now."

Labeling or Name-Calling

One way to differentiate children is by labeling or giving them special names. Too often, however, labels and pet names are stereotyped by culture or gender and adversely affect children's self-beliefs and independence; moreover, they are usually single-dimensional, which belies the fact that all of us have multiple talents to nurture.[14]

Since children do not usually separate themselves from their behavior or from labels attached to behavior, name-calling can become a self-fulfilling prophecy. Even friendly nicknames or seemingly positive labels can be highly restrictive to a child's growth and learning. Early and incorrect labeling can act like frost on a budding plant. Certain abilities and interests may not be tested in the growing-up process, and natural talents may wither if not nurtured or given space. Try taking the perspective of an interested naturalist who observes and waits to see how children's inborn temperament is expressed.

Follow up on children's enthusiastic actions and interests, and expose them to a wide variety of opportunities, places, people, and ideas. Such efforts will help adults and children live together in the light of acceptance and equality. With this approach, the light of appreciation and enjoyment grows for all participants. Here are some suggestions for avoiding labels:

1. At times, your child may unconsciously remind you of your own least favorite trait.

    Heavy/Unwelcoming: "She is so disorganized. Her room is a pigpen. I guess I'm like that when I have a lot going on, but I crack the whip with her to make her get organized. She hates it, but she does it when I get on her."
    Or: "Quit acting like a prima donna. People can't stand you when you act like you're the only one in the room. You should respect me when we go out in public."

    Light/Welcoming: "We're a lot alike in some ways, although we are different, too. She has such a creative streak, and she's always working on so many projects. We have to work to tolerate each other's messiness, since neither of us likes to clean up or throw out stuff we think we can use."

2. Due to unresolved issues with other family members, your child's normal behavior may seem highly undesirable.

    Heavy/Unwelcoming: "He's the difficult one—he takes after my brother, who was the family brat. Both of them are stubborn as mules, only doing what they want to. I can tell him something a dozen times, but he never listens—especially when he's reading or using the computer. They both make me so angry and tired."

Light/Welcoming: "Jared is a lot like my younger brother in one way. Both of them are very emotionally intense in their likes and dislikes. They both get totally absorbed in something of interest to them for a long, long time. They don't want to be interrupted at all."

Or: "Jared, I know it's hard to be interrupted when you're so absorbed, but we need to leave in ten minutes. I know you heard me, and I set the clock timer for a five-minute reminder so we can leave on time."

3. Typecasting children in a tight mold encourages either passive acceptance of that label or painful rebellion against it. Even positive labeling and boasting can cause a strong sense of inferiority and the feeling that they cannot make mistakes or explore anything unknown.

Heavy/Unwelcoming: "Michael is our scholar. We knew he was brilliant when he began teething earlier than other children. His grandparents started an Ivy League university fund for him on his second birthday. He'd rather study than be with people. He'll make us all proud someday."

Light/Welcoming: "Michael, we've always been proud of you for so many reasons. You've been dedicated to your academic work. What would you think of branching out, doing something not related to school or grades? How about trying the world of music as your favorite cousin, Carolyn, did? Or, you could try helping Uncle Brian with some volunteer work at the shelter. You get along well with both of them. What do you think?"

4. Try to avoid making the child feel unidimensional by expecting achievement in only one area or seeing a limited potential or range of personality traits. Also, avoid comparing family members and expecting them to travel a similar, prescribed path.

Heavy/Unwelcoming: "I always wanted a kid who got along with people, and here she is, Miss Popularity. She'll do anything to be the best-liked girl in every situation."

Or: "All my kids are jocks! With all the time they spend at the gym, they better get athletic scholarships to college. My stepson is Mr. Mathematician—always so serious and logical. He'll go far because he always toes the line. He never rocks the boat."

Light/Welcoming: "All the kids are so different, each with individual strengths. It would be so easy to label each one, but I don't allow anyone to pigeonhole them. I know each of the kids will find so many things to interest and challenge them as they grow up. It's truly an adventure to help each one find their own special path."

In the following true example, the adult shares some of her own biography with a child, giving special credit to those who continually supported her with her growth pattern and path. This light and welcoming technique can be very effective and liberating in helping children risk testing hidden talents and exploring multidimensional possibilities in an ever-changing world. Knowing on a deep level that one person believes in you and will continue to love you sends a powerful message that life is a journey and a process to be personally explored and shared with others.

I know you are struggling in this family (or at school) to find out who you are. I went through a similar period when I was your age, and I see you wondering how you are different from others. Well, I want you to know that I believe in you and will support you when you work hard at following your passions. I'm so grateful that my mother trusted me and gave me love and freedom to be my own person—to try out different areas. She didn't label any of us in the family. I knew she would always believe in me whatever I decided to do in life. I have always felt her love and light in my life, and I still do.

Playing Together to Build, Rebuild, and Heal Relationships

Trusting oneself and others is basic in all healthy relationships. Children who operate from a secure and solid basis of trust can build mutuality and connectedness with others; they want to communicate, collaborate, and co-create with adults and peers. This translates into hope for the immediate future and a generalized faith in a sense of order that somehow things will work out.[15]

When trust is broken, we need to honestly and systematically rebuild the relationship. Children who have been shamed and made to feel unnecessarily guilty for being themselves need to be healed so they can embrace life. Additionally, mutual forgiveness between adults and children needs to be deeply experienced if there has been painful name-calling and restrictive labeling.

Fortunately, enjoying Mother Nature, the arts, literature, and playing and laughing together are natural relationship healers and builders. Play is the working partner of growth and a nonthreatening context for interaction of all types for all ages.[16] The fun and laughter that result create lightheartedness and open up unique opportunities for connecting and co-creating meaning and purpose. Playing together can unexpectedly and joyfully flow into celebrating life and one another's existence together.

All the following play materials and activities can be tried out in an all-play, no-fail, no-competition atmosphere, with control being equally shared by all participants.

1. Infants and toddlers (birth to three years):

- Provide a rocking chair with pillows and stuffed animals for cuddling.
- Play friendly peek-a-boo and hide-and-chase partner games. Involve stuffed animals and family pets in the fun.
- Play with water toys (strainers, funnels, cups, or boats) in a plastic dishpan or portable pool. Add blue or green food coloring for different effects.
- Read and enjoy: *Goodnight Moon*,[17] *Jamberry*,[18] *Barnyard Dance*,[19] *Babybug* magazine, *I Love My Mommy Because . . .*,[20] and *I Love My Daddy Because. . . .*[21]

2. Three to six years:

- Play-act, for the children's benefit, parts of *The Three Little Kittens*, *Goldilocks and The Three Bears*, or a favorite story. Invite, but do not insist on, the children's participation.
- Sing favorite silly, beloved songs such as "Old MacDonald," "If You're Happy," or "Down by the Bay."
- Do the "Bunny Hop" or "Hokey Pokey" together.
- Make up an animal dance such as the "Lizard Leap," "Froggy Hop," or "Kangaroo Highhop."
- Build a structure with wet sand or Play Dough™.
- Read and enjoy: *The Tale of Peter Rabbit*,[22] *The Lady with the Alligator Purse*,[23] *The Temper Tantrum Book*,[24] or *The Little Engine That Could*.[25]

- Listen to the audio tapes of Raffi's "Baby Beluga" songs,[26] "A Twinkle in Your Eye" by Burl Ives,[27] or *Winnie the Pooh*[28] read by Charles Kuralt.

3. Seven to eleven years:

- Cooperatively build with a Blockhead™ game set.
- Cooperatively create with a Magna Doodle™, Spirograph™, or Etch-a-Sketch™.
- Watch a nature video or a *National Geographic* special together.
- Read "knock-knock"[29] and riddle joke books together (choose from the hilarious collections by Joseph Rosenbloom[30] or Katy Hall and Lisa Eisenberg[31]).
- Read and play-act your favorite parts of *The Berenstain Bears* and *The Messy Room*,[32] *The Berenstain Bears and Too Much TV*,[33] or *The Berenstain Bears and Too Much Junk Food*.[34]
- Read and enjoy *Charlotte's Web*,[35] or listen to it on audiocassette, read by the author, E. B. White.[36]
- Read and enjoy *James Herriot's Treasury for Children*,[37] based on the English veterinarian's life.
- Read *Children Just Like Me*;[38] *Fathers, Mothers, Sisters, Brothers: A Collection of Family Poems*;[39] or *The Wizard Of Oz*;[40] or watch the 1939 movie on video together.
- Watch *The Wishbone* (dog) *Classics* series on PBS.
- Watch the videos *ET, Babe,* or *Homeward Bound.*
- Listen to the audiocassette of *Ramona Forever,*[41] read by Stockard Channing, or *The Story of Dr. Doolittle,*[42] read by Alan Bennett.

4. Twelve years through the teen years:

- Walk with a pet, or feed animals in a nature area.
- Play Koosh™ ball, using only your feet or little fingers.
- Pantomime an embarrassing secret such as wearing two different-colored shoes or forgetting your own name.
- Act out feelings of hilarity, disappointment, anger, sadness, pride of accomplishment, or being misunderstood.
- Play solitaire together on the computer.
- Read aloud the comics section in the newspaper.
- Read and enjoy silly and stimulating wordplay rhymes from *Walking the Bridge of Your Nose*.[43]
- Read Kathleen Krull's biographies filled with quirky tidbits: *Lives of the Athletes, Lives of the Artists, Lives of the Musicians, Lives of the Writers (And What the Neighbors Thought)*.[44]
- Take turns reading aloud from the autobiography of an admired person.
- Watch the videos *Apollo 13, Shiloh, The Amazing Panda Adventure*, or *To Kill A Mockingbird*.
- Listen to the audiocassette of *A Wrinkle in Time*,[45] written and read by Madeleine L'Engle.

An Indigo's Grace

The Dalai Lama was speaking before a group. He was told that a child with cancer wanted to see him, and he immediately asked the child to come onto the stage with him. Flashing the effervescent smile that is his natural trademark, the Dalai Lama respectfully asked the child to tell the audience whatever was on his mind. Without hesitation, the child turned, faced the crowd, and said: "I am a child with cancer, but I am a child first. I need to play. I need to laugh. I need you to see my heart's joy. Then, you may see that my body has cancer."

This simple story has profound meaning for the Indigo Children as well. Yes, they are different. Yes, they are old souls. Yes, they have special purposes. Yes, they are inspired. Yes, they have special talents and abilities. Yes, yes, yes: but they are children first and foremost. Let us remember this, and we can better nurture their special nature.

The special nature of the Indigo Child requires special discipline techniques. Below, Robert Gerard gives us more of his thoughts and guidelines:

Disciplining the Indigo Child
Robert Gerard, Ph.D.

Discipline is extremely vital for the Indigo Child. Since they are very creative and alert, they try things out and explore their boundaries. They want to be reassured, to know the safety limits, and to be informed about which life experiences do not serve their highest good. I often see parents "telling" their children what to do or not do. This stifles their creativity and suppresses expression. They will retort, becoming defensive and obnoxious.

I've coined the term *loving discipline* to connote how I process disciplinary action with the intent of serving the child's spiritual interests. Loving discipline follows these guidelines:

1. Keep the child informed and involved.
2. Prevent potential misunderstanding by simple explanations.
3. Don't react to your child.
4. Avoid issuing orders.
5. Keep your word.
6. Deal with each situation in the moment.
7. No hitting or use of abusive language.
8. Let your emotion show love.
9. If a reprimand is given, make it a "time-out" event.
10. Talk the situation over after the reprimand.
11. Afterward, always join together and ascertain that all is smoothed out.

The big surprise is that your child will respect you for your wisdom and foresight in allowing their Indigo energy to thrive! I allow my daughter, Samara, abundant freedom and creativity, but rarely does she escape my strict watch over her attitude and behavior. On the surface, I appear to be too tough, but Samara knows my limits and thresholds, and when I discipline her, she invariably thanks me for dealing with her situation.

"Overparenting" is a big no-no. Deep down inside, many parents fear abandonment and loss of their children's love. These parents go out of their way to win favor by overindulging and pacifying their child. Once the child realizes that he or she can control the adult's behavior, they will. If allowed, an Indigo may step into the parental role. This complicates the relationship and forces the child to acquire the shortcomings of the parent and not live in their own present.

Parents need to keep conscious of their relationship with Indigo Children. Maybe the advice given to me by a clairvoyant should be shared here: "Robert, your daughter needs guidance, love, and discipline, not parents. She knows her purpose and mission. Be her guide." That guidance has helped me enormously.

Education and the Indigo Child

> One had to cram all of this stuff into one's mind, whether one liked it or not. This coercion had such a deterring effect that, after I had passed the final examination, I found the consideration of any scientific problems distasteful to me for an entire year. . . . It is in fact nothing short of a miracle that the modern methods of instruction have not entirely strangled the holy spirit of inquiry; for this delicate little plant, aside from stimulation, stands mainly in need of freedom; without this it goes to wrack and ruin without fail. It is a very grave mistake to think that the enjoyment of seeing and searching can be promoted by means of coercion and a sense of duty.
> — Albert Einstein

What can we say to you about education? In a nutshell, it *must* change to accommodate the Indigo Children. Much of this will come about due to incredible frustration on the part of teachers, who are crying out for the system to pay attention and shift accordingly. Some of the change may come about due to the eventual realization that test scores are actually low because the kids are reacting to the tests, and not because they are low in their thinking and awareness skills. This will have the effect of making education planners, managers, and psychologists ask if the consciousness of the teaching and training fits the tests (one of the most important questions to look at).

The following discussions are from educators who are sharply focused on the problem. After that, we present some information regarding alternate schooling that is working for Indigos. Finally, we offer some alternate methods to help the children—new methods that are working on difficult children.

All of this is our effort to give you hope: You don't simply have to turn your kids over to the current system and walk away. There are things you can do and places you can go. Is this effort worth it? You bet!

We want you to meet **Robert P. Ocker**. He is a middle-school guidance counselor for the school district of Mondovi, Wisconsin. A merchant of hope and an agent of change, his passion and purpose for most of his life has been to guide youth. He has given numerous presentations to audiences of all ages. He helps students focus on problem solving, conflict resolution, taking responsibility, and character education. He was recognized by the Wisconsin School Counselors Association as one of the most outstanding future educational leaders. As far as we are concerned, Robert is "right on!"

A Heart-Centered Journey:
An Educational Vision for Paradigm Pioneers
Robert P. Ocker

In education and child raising, we are now reaching a crucial turning point, a moment of paradigm shift. There is a general sense that the question of how to raise and educate our kids is the most profound question facing us today. Education requires a new vision for the children of the 21st century, offering hope and inspiration to the children of the world. This vision can be found in the children's dreams. We need a comprehensive understanding of human life in order to practice a true and comprehensive pedagogy that will serve humanity in the new millennium—that humanity which is, of course, today's children. The kids are worth it, and our future depends on it.

Educators must admit that, just as we demand that the present social structure be transformed, we must also demand that the art of education be transformed so that it flows from a different wellspring. Of course, we *can* transform it—for the art of education depends on the educators.

We must develop a new understanding of human nature and offer our guidance based on that. We must give our children and students the gift of guidance toward inner discipline and peace.

We must truly perceive children's natures as they develop and allow them to develop themselves as human beings. They must choose how their nature and essence will mature into adulthood.

The educators of the 21st century will come to know and guide the developing human being, giving the gift of inner discipline. With wit and wisdom, we will guide children of character to become responsible, resourceful, and caring individuals.

Therefore, as educators, we need to become paradigm pioneers—we must revisit our assumptions about the meaning, purpose, and function of education, and come to a new awareness. We must teach children *how* to think, not *what* to think. Our role is not to pass on *knowledge*, but rather *wisdom*. Wisdom is knowledge applied. When we only give children knowledge, we are telling them what to think, what they are supposed to know, and what we want them to believe is true.

When we give children wisdom, however, we do not tell them what to know or what is true—rather, we tell them how to get their own truth. Of course, we cannot ignore knowledge when teaching wisdom, because without knowledge there is no wisdom. A certain amount of knowledge must be passed on from one generation to the next, but we must let children discover for themselves! Knowledge is often lost, but wisdom is never forgotten.

I envision an educational system based upon developing children's *abilities and skills* rather than their *memories*. Children are our guides; we should give them the ability to discover and create their own truths. Critical thinking, problem solving, imagination, honesty, and responsibility must become the crux of education for the children of the 21st century.

My vision of the future of education is based on unconditional love. This is the essence of the new human being. We, the educators, must be sure to surround ourselves with colleagues who have the heart and soul to raise the children of today to be the people of tomorrow. A real education will take care of the body, soul, and spirit, which will be intrinsically free and independent. A real education must care to put people into life. Educators will perform a great service to humanity if we are pioneers in this respect. We must renew the educational system for the betterment of humanity. If you take part in this heart-centered journey, the children will be blessed, and so will the whole future of humanity.

We are going to hear from Robert again, but now we want you to meet **Cathy Patterson,** a special education teacher in Canada. Like Debra Hegerle and Robert Ocker, she has daily experience with children in an educational venue. Cathy, however, is part of the management of special programs for problem children. She offers her comments and remarks for our benefit.

Strategies to Use in
Guiding Indigo Children
Cathy Patterson

I am a special education teacher who operates a program within the educational system designed to serve students with severe behavior disorders. As you can imagine, I have worked with several students with genuine attention deficits and various emotional disturbances throughout the years, and have provided support to their teachers and parents.

However, I have also experienced a definite number of children who were *labeled* ADD or ADHD, yet who no longer required medication once their emotional needs were met at home and at school. Also, I have met students *assumed* to be ADHD by their teachers and doctors, until they started responding to various behavioral strategies at home and school. I believe that if students respond to such interventions, then the diagnosis of ADHD is inaccurate.

Of course, there are children who are truly ADHD, possibly due to neurological imbalances or even brain damage, and they cannot function at all without proper medication. These true ADHD students may not all be Indigo Children, and they respond more favorably to medication than to behavior interventions because they have very little, if any, impulse control.

In the following section, I would like to discuss some of the new energy changes that I have witnessed within the education system, as well as some of the problems and old energy patterns around discipline that are affecting many emotionally disturbed children. Many of these children are probably Indigos. Finally, I will conclude by offering practical strategies for parents and teachers to support and empower children, while still providing them with necessary guidelines and boundaries.

The old energy patterns in schools are based on the fundamental belief that children are empty vessels who are to be filled with knowledge by the expert, the teacher. In the traditional system, students learn how to be contributing members of our society by learning everything needed for employment. They demonstrate listening skills and learn self-worth based on how much quality written output they produce. The teacher uses shaming techniques and compares students to each other, which is supposed to motivate students to produce even more written output. In this atmosphere, any child who does not unquestioningly conform is considered to have problems.

Fortunately, contemporary educators have developed numerous techniques and strategies that are more student-centered, such as self-evaluation, self-directed individual education plans, portfolio assessment, and student-led conferencing. For example, elementary schoolteachers in British Columbia no longer use grades of F for Failure. Instead, they use IP, meaning "in progress," to signify that the student is taking a little longer to complete course objectives. The teacher must then develop a plan for how the child will meet those objectives.

Some educators have also introduced programs that empower children and validate their abilities as leaders, including peer mediation, peer counselors, and bully-proofing programs. Also, parents are playing a more active role in schools by joining Parent Advisory Committees (PACs) in order to develop fund-raising activities for the school. Parent volunteers are also becoming active members of primary classrooms.

One the of the last vestiges of the old energy in schools has to do with the discipline methods used. Unfortunately, many children are still being sent out in the hallway when they are not compliant, and then being sent to the office where the principal gives them a lecture about behaving. The next step is being sent home. The problem with this system is that children learn to meet their needs for attention and recognition in negative ways. They soon learn to enjoy the attention they receive while out into the hallway. The giggling and pointing gives them the peer recognition they crave—everybody knows their name, especially if this happens frequently.

From birth, Indigo Children have a need for recognition and status. If not handled properly, these children can learn to meet these needs at the cost of losing an education. They will quickly notice if they have the power to make adults yell and scream with just one little smirk. They really can be like royalty, with all this attention! Furthermore, if they are sent home, that is the best reward since they don't have to complete schoolwork, and may even get to watch TV or play video games.

Parents would probably be horrified by the amount of time children spend out in the hallways of schools. They may be sent out with schoolwork, but these unsupervised children are busy getting their peers' attention by making faces or the like.

Many students move to the high school level with significant gaps in learning because of the amount of time they spend in the hallways of our schools. Also, many children come from transient homes, and they have even greater learning gaps. Some of these students leave the seventh grade without the ability to read!

These old discipline practices are starting to change. I strongly believe that parents are an integral part of this change. Parents need to begin asking schools about their discipline practices, and they need to question whether their child's needs are being met. I am currently on a committee that is examining alternative strategies, interventions, and support for students. We are no longer part of the traditional system in which children are strange, irregular, or disordered if they do not sit quietly in class, and the only alternative is for them to be sent home or to a special education program.

Are Your Children's Needs Being Met at School?

Children need safety, attention, respect, dignity, and a secure place where they belong. The following questions can help parents decide whether these needs are being met at school. I have also included some helpful strategies along the way.

1. Does your child's school have a schoolwide discipline plan? Do they send children out into the hallway and then home for suspensions as a solution to behavioral problems? If so, suggest alternatives.

2. What is the atmosphere of your child's classroom? Is students' work displayed on the walls? Does the teacher greet the children with respect? Does the teacher praise the students and have a positive focus?

3. Does the teacher have positive ways to give students power and responsibility, such as having student helpers, special chores, a hall of fame, and sharing circles?

4. Are students part of the decision-making process? Are there student-led conferences, student councils, or class meetings? Can students make class rules?

5. Is there a structure to the classroom? Do the children know their responsibilities and the teacher's expectations?

6. Does the teacher break up tasks into parts and not overwhelm students with directions? Students with attention difficulties need to have one step at a time, and they may need a visual sign, such as a chart with stars, showing how much time they have left on a task. Once they have so many stars, they can get free time, or time to work on another project of their choice.

7. Do the children know the purpose of their task? If the child asks why they are doing something, does the teacher provide a friendly explanation, or only consequences?

8. Do students have breaks during the day so that they are not always sitting at their desks doing work?

9. Is the material interesting and appropriate? Can the students do separate reports or write up information in different ways but still learn about the same material?

10. If students are having difficulties understanding the material, does the teacher adapt or modify the material so that they can complete the work along with the rest of the class?

11. Are the teacher's expectations clear and consistent? Is there a regular set of consequences for not following the classroom rules, or do these rules change depending on the teacher's mood?

12. Is the structure of the classroom constantly changing, or do the students know ahead of time what types of work will be expected during the day?

13. If children are not paying attention in class, are they moved away from whoever or whatever is distracting them, such as other children, door entrances, or windows? Are they still a part of the classroom activities, or do they feel ashamed and disconnected from the class?

14. If the child misbehaves, is there a plan in place for a structured time-out in another supervised setting, or is the child sent out into the hallway?

15. Do the teacher and school staff try to take the emotion out of disciplining? Ensure that they are not incessantly yelling at children or giving them excessive lectures on behaving, because this will only feed the children's need for attention and recognition in negative ways.

16. Is the child simply referred to as "bad," or does the school staff instead discuss the "poor choices" that the child has made? Does the staff make comments such as these to the student: "Was this a good choice? What could you have done differently? What would be a better choice?"

17. Does the teacher report only on the problems and not focus on positive behavior?

18. Are there some visual signs around the classroom which show how well students are doing, such as star charts, graphs, or certificates?

19. Does the teacher show the child alternative ways of dealing with conflict, and self-talk strategies?

20. Does your child have an opportunity to earn privileges in the classroom for following directions and focusing on their work? Does the teacher have a token economy system in place? If not, inquire as to how one could be set up for your child or the entire class.

21. Do you have a communication book that the teacher signs every day so that you consistently know how your child is doing at school and are aware of positive changes as well? Examine this book daily, and have positive discussions with your child about their behavior at school.

22. What is your view of education? Is it important? Are you supportive of the school staff? Do you dislike your child's teacher? Have you made criticisms about this teacher in front of your child?

Are Your Children's Needs Being Met at Home?

The following questions can help you make sure that the home atmosphere supports your children and nurtures all their gifts.

1. Do you feel that your children's opinions are valuable, and that you can learn from them? Or do you always have to do the teaching and lecturing in this relationship?

2. Do you listen to your children and have a lot of fun together? Do you make time for your inner kids to play together?

3. Do you respect their privacy and personal space?

4. Do you give reasons why you make certain decisions?

5. Do you frequently praise your child, and offer three compliments for every criticism?

6. Can you sometimes admit that you made a mistake and are sorry?

7. Do you teach your child to have respect and compassion for other people?

8. Do you take time to teach your children about different aspects of the world, such as why we need

rain? Do you listen as they try to tell you about their view of the world? Listen to their explanations even if you already know this information.

9. Do you frequently encourage your children, or do you instead tell them why they will never be able to complete a certain task?

10. Do you do things for your children that they can do for themselves?

11. Do you give your children responsibilities around the house, and give them a choice of these responsibilities?

12. Do you overcorrect your children? If so, only correct them on the really important issues. Is it really important that your child has correct posture every minute of the day? Don't sweat the small stuff.

13. Do you notice when your children behave and then praise them for it?

14. Do you have regular family meetings in order to discuss who has certain responsibilities then and what fun family outings will soon occur? Do your children play an important role during these meetings, and are they part of the decision-making process? During family meetings, you can even agree together on consequences for certain misbehavior, and/or privileges for behaving.

15. Do you teach your children about different emotions and ways of communicating these emotions, or are some emotions never to be expressed?

16. Do you listen to your children when they complain about being lonely or depressed, or feeling isolated?

Or do you dismiss their feelings as a passing phase?

17. Do you have clear and consistent expectations and consequences for when your children misbehave?

18. Are you feeding your children excessive amounts of sugar and preservatives? Do they have any allergies or show any sign of hyperactivity after eating certain foods?

Setting Boundaries and Guidelines

Parents do not help their children by explaining that they are "Indigo Children" and then allowing them to misbehave without boundaries and guidelines. Even children who could eventually raise the consciousness of the planet need boundaries. With boundaries, self-control is learned, which is integral for a peaceful community. The Indigo Child needs to be corrected and given boundaries using a method that represents the new energy. The following suggestions are effective strategies that provide discipline while still preserving the child's dignity:

1. When giving directions, you can phrase them as, "I need you to help me by moving your shoes out of the doorway, please." The key is stating, "I need you to help me . . ."

2. Advise children that they are going to need to get ready for an activity such as dinner in a couple of minutes.

3. Give children as much choice as possible. If they usually do not want to come to the dinner table, tell them they have a choice of coming in one minute or two minutes. Do not deviate from the

choices provided if they are only trying to be difficult. If they offer another alternative that is logical, such as asking if they can come to the table after they clean up their game, then agree to it.

4. Provide short explanations as to why you want things done.

5. Give one direction at a time so that they are not overwhelmed by too many directions.

6. Sit with the children and decide on certain consequences for negative behaviors. For example, say: "You have a habit of leaving your toys around the house and I trip over them. What can we do about this? Can you help me decide what should happen if you don't clean up your toys?" Follow these pre-set consequences.

7. Set up a time-out chair or quiet area in your home where children must go when they have consequences. Children should not be simply sent to their room if it is full of stimulating toys that they will be playing with while in the room.

8. When you need to give warning for misbehavior, you can use Phelan's 1-2-3 Magic System: Make a request for the children to stop a certain behavior, then give them a count of three to stop. If you count to three and they haven't stopped the behavior, then they get a time-out.

9. Take the emotion out of discipline by not lecturing or arguing with your child. Provide the necessary consequences: "Tommy, I am not going to argue with you. It is not okay for you to hit other people, and I want you to have a time-out now. You need to go to the quiet chair now." Focus on the conse-

quences, and act almost indifferent. You must be careful not to hug them during this time. This is a boundary, and children need to learn that every action has a consequence.

If they scream and act disruptive, then you should add time by calculating on your watch or by placing checks on a piece of paper. You should not argue; instead, say something like, "I'll start your time-out when you are ready and I am time." When the time-out is over, remember to ask your children to explain why they had a time-out.

10. You may even want to have star charts or graphs at home on the fridge so that when children behave during a set amount of time, they get a star or a check, When they have enough stars or checks, then they get extra privileges, such as going on a special outing. This is a positive way to focus on behavior.

11. Remember to notice when your children are behaving, and praise them for following your expectations: "I am pleased that you . . ." or "It is nice that you . . ."

12. Ask your child to repeat a behavior properly: "Tommy, it is not okay to run into the house with your muddy shoes on. Can you please show me how you can do it again properly?" Tommy takes his shoes off. "Thank you, I knew you could do it. That's better."

13. Children feel more secure with regular routines, and they respond better if they have regular eating, sleeping, and leisure times.

14. Remember to always be consistent even if you feel that you don't have the energy to follow your discipline plan. Otherwise, children learn that they don't need to follow rules, because those rules are always changing.

I hope that this information is helpful. I encourage parents to ensure that schools are accountable for providing support to emotionally disruptive children instead of following outdated discipline practices. Also, I believe that parents should examine their own attitudes toward their children to ensure that they are respectful and are providing opportunities for empowerment. Finally, parents need to establish the boundaries and guidelines that are necessary for their children's growth and development. The strategies listed above are particularly useful for Indigo Children because they are able to preserve their own sense of relevance and to be treated with dignity.

On a more personal note, here is **Robert Ocker** again, an educator in love with children of all ages:

Honoring the Little Ones As Gifts
Robert P. Ocker

Giving a lesson on conflict resolution to kindergarten kids in Eau Claire, Wisconsin, I reached out and asked the class, "What is violence, boys and girls?" A beautiful girl with the stars sparkling in her eyes replied, "That's easy—they are beautiful purple flowers [violets!]. I smell them every day, and they make me happy."

My soul radiated with love and peace. Her energy sent wisdom and strength. As our eyes connected in her sea of stars, I said, "Keep smelling your flowers, Little One. You understand peace. And I was wondering if you would like to teach the class about fear. We can do it together, as friends." She just smiled and took my hand. She was a gift.

The new Indigo kids—I refer to them as Little Ones—have come here to give us a new understanding of humanity. They are gifts to their parents, the planet, and the universe. When we honor the Little Ones as gifts, we see the divine wisdom they bring to help raise the vibration of planet Earth.

The single most important step to understanding and communicating with the new kids is to change your thinking about them. By shifting your paradigm to honor the little ones as gifts instead of problems, you will open the door to understanding their wisdom as well as your own. The Little Ones will honor your intent, and the gateway to understanding will be unwrapped. Every child that enters your life has come to you to receive a gift. In doing so, the Little One gives a gift to you—the gift of experiencing and fulfilling Who You Are.

Living Instinctually

Working with kids of all age groups (kindergarten through 12th grade), I noticed that first graders seem to understand more than adults do. They trust their instincts and intuition. I was talking about communication to first-grade students, when I was awakened by the gift of an Indigo boy. We were discussing how important it was to listen.

This wonderful boy gently walked up to me and said with such wisdom, "Mr. Ocker, *listen* and *silent* are the same word, only they have different letters." I smiled and felt his brilliance. As we looked at each other, we said nothing but understood everything. He taught me by his instinctual words the wisest sort of communication.

Indigo Children live instinctually. This is a difficult process for the Little Ones, who are both caught in, and agents of, humanity's transition to living instinctually. The Little Ones are challenged daily, because in many cultures instinctual input is ignored. The dominant cultures mistrust it so deeply, in fact, that children are taught from their earliest years to fear their instincts.

Young people intuitively sense that their ego can be a positive aspect of their personality, and is in fact necessary to effectively manage their affairs. Our culture reinforces this sense. Yet, and this is where the Indigo kids become confused and frustrated, we teach the new kids that it's wrong to listen to their egos, and that they must develop social personae as protective veneers. Then, they retreat in safety behind these images, forever after pursuing physical-plane relationships from behind that mask. Educational systems, the media, and culturally adjusted persons teach that developing a "self-image" is an urgent matter of grave importance. This creates a poison for the new kids.

Such acculturated children look always to others—parents, teachers, and authority figures—for guidance, direction, and an understanding of reality. Often these children stay in this outward orientation for the rest of their lives, assigning so little value to the inner voice of spirit that soon their instincts are all but forgotten. Like others in our sleepwalking society, they begin calculating their life values using unwieldy and often anxiety-permeated processes of reasoning. This is the only measure of success they are taught to value.

This season's children offer new consciousness about self-image. They bring to the planet a new understanding about humanity and a vision of living instinctually. They want to live spontaneously, instinctually—to simply be! They want to say the right words without thinking of them ahead of time, and to experience the purity of a mind uncluttered by troublesome and misplaced responsibility. They want to know the right gesture, the right behavior, and the creative response for each and every situation. This is the vision of humanity they teach us. They cry for us to trust our selves, our instincts, and our intuitive senses. These are the birthrights of each and every human being.

With the proper guidance, the Indigo Children will mature—not only retaining this ability, but developing it, honing it to a fine art. They and their societies will live instinctually from moment to moment, as they are inviting us to live now.

Discipline Without Punishment

Punishment will not work with these kids. It establishes fear, requires judgment, creates intentions of anger, and invites more conflict. These children will withdraw, rebel, and sink inward with hate. This is dangerous for their souls and for the lives of others. Avoid punishment!

Discipline guides children by providing logical and realistic consequences. It shows what they have done wrong, gives them ownership of the problem, offers them ways to solve the problem they created, and leaves their dignity intact.

Experiencing logical and realistic consequences teaches the Indigo Child that they have positive control over their lives and that they can make decisions and solve their own problems. The children want this guidance. It empowers their royal and wise nature and gives them the power to be responsible, resourceful, and caring individuals. It allows them to be Who They Are!

These children demand dignity and worth. They read your intent more than your words. They are wise in their souls, young in their hearts. Treat them with the same respect and responsibility you would treat yourself. They will honor you for this guidance. They will understand, by your ethic of care and intent of compassion, that to share your love with them is to love yourself and celebrate the place where we are all One. Therefore, say what you mean, mean what you say, and do what you said you would do. Let integrity guide you! Model these messages for the Little Ones, and they will grow into seeds of joy.

Choices are a very important part of discipline and empowerment. If you want these kids to make wise choices, give them the opportunity to make lots of choices—including some unwise ones. Unless the unwise ones are life threatening, morally threatening, or unhealthy, allow them to experience the real-world consequences of their own mistakes and poor choices, as painful as they may be.

Some of the best research into working with kids and effective concepts about working with children (and all people) has been done by Foster Cline, M.D., and Jim Fay, in *Parenting with Love and Logic*.[46] These principles work with children! These authors are paradigm pioneers, dealing with what is happening with kids today and how to fix it. I highly recommend their work.

Just for Teachers

Many, many schoolteachers we meet are asking the same question: "What can I do within the system to help the Indigo Children? I can't effect change, and I feel that my hands are tied! I'm frustrated!"

Jennifer Palmer is a teacher in Australia. Like teachers all over the world, she must work within the system, yet she is very aware of the new aspects of Indigo Children. Jennifer has a diploma in teaching, and a graduate certificate in education. With 23 years of experience, this is how she deals with Indigos in her classroom.

Teaching the Children
Jennifer Palmer

In our classroom, we take time to discuss what the students expect, including what they expect from their teacher. This usually blows them away. They soon discover that what they expect from me goes both ways, and as a result they begin to see why we as teachers expect certain things from them as well. They begin to see the equality and rights of each party.

We have to live together for a year as a family. It is better that we all agree on the ground rules so that everyone knows what is expected of them. My class rules feature more expectations and rights than traditional rules.

Consequences are built on the nature of the offense, instead of just having them for their own sake, devoid of relevance. All statements are positive: Terms such as *no* and *don't* are not used. The whole thing can take a week to design, think about, and put into place, compared to the old quick list of "do's and don'ts," unchanged for decades. But through this effort, we all expect to have fun and grow personally to the best of our ability at the time.

I share events in my life that may impact on my relationship with the students, such as whether I'm unwell, have lost something, am injured, have a headache, or share a common interest in a sport. Likewise, if they are upset, they need to express it so that everyone else understands. We share and support each other.

I'm available as a listener, not a "tattletale," unless I'm given permission to share with appropriate people. I can be their friend and confidante.

The Curriculum

Individuals are catered to and programmed for according to varying needs, where possible and according to skills and knowledge.

Topics, themes, and units of work are devised for our activities: for example, group work, self-assessment, reviewing literature, and researching aids. Students are sometimes involved in selecting topics and certainly have choice, within set parameters, to pursue areas of interest.

This offers a wide range of complexity and high-level thinking, and caters to varying learning styles. Often students who would traditionally have received special support choose the higher-level thinking tasks as well.

Although there is an enormous amount of work in the preparation, the outcomes far outweigh the cost. Activities are designed to teach both simple and complex thinking, and include:

- observing;
- grouping, classifying;
- restating, remembering, reviewing;
- comparing, contrasting;
- comprehending, understanding;
- reasoning, judging;
- applying;
- designing; and
- creating.

Assessment can be done by oneself, peers, or the teacher; it can take different forms such as learning logs, presentation, posters, demonstrations, role-playing, product analysis, selected/specific criteria, written anecdotal notes, conferences, or filmed diaries. Students often negotiate these, and if the teacher has selected what is being assessed, students are certainly informed at task commencement. Collaborative learning is a useful, effective, and popular methodology employed by teachers today.

This is a fairly brief description of how I work in schools as a co-creator and facilitator of children's learning and personal development.

Alternate Schooling for Indigo Children

Following are descriptions of two existing worldwide alternate schooling systems for Indigo Children. By "alternate," we mean a choice that differs from existing systems that are failing to see the changing needs of the new children. Often the latter are publicly run by the city. Not all public schools are inadequate for Indigos though, and we have actually seen tremendous changes of awareness in isolated (usually smaller) towns due to an advanced-thinking superintendent, or a system that allows the teachers great flexibility. We celebrate these efforts, but this is not the norm. You as a parent can tell a lot about your child's school using the points that Cathy Patterson presented a few pages earlier.

Ultimately, we'd like to have a list of schools all over the world, listed by country and city. After looking at the following, you might angrily say, "How could you possibly have excluded this or that school?" We admit that we are just beginning, and only know a few of them. That's why this book is an *introductory* book on the subject. We have, however, provided a way for you to view *new* information *now*. You can use our website at **www.Indigochild.com** as an addendum to this book.

This is where you can effect change: If you feel there are some existing systems that we should have included, or you have information about wonderful Indigo-type schools in your city, go ahead and write to us. On our website, we will list new information regarding alternate Indigo-type schools all over the world. If your suggestion is viable, then we will include it on the website. Then it will be available to parents instantly, instead of waiting for another book! This is where the Internet's usefulness really shines. We really do want everyone to be able to see the latest information, and we are not promoting any certain schools for any commercial reason.

What kind of school would be an alternative, you might ask? The answer is a school that follows the patterns and suggestions set forth here. Do such schools exist? Yes, and many have existed for some time . . . even before the Indigo phenomenon.

The main attributes of such schools are easy to spot and very fundamental. They are as follows:

1. The students are honored—not the system.

2. The students are offered reasonable choice regarding *how* the lessons are presented, and at what speed.

3. The curriculum is flexible from class to class, often changing based on who is doing the learning in a certain group.

4. The children and teachers—not the system—are responsible for setting the learning standards.

5. Teachers have great autonomy within their own student groups.

6. Old educational paradigms are not worshiped. New ideas are welcome.

7. Tests are constantly changed and reworked to fit the students' skills and awareness as well as the information being taught and absorbed. (Nothing is worse than very bright children taking old tests that are far beneath them. They often will misunderstand or discard them mentally, and therefore fail them. The tests must evolve with the student's awareness.)

8. A constantly changing way of doing things is the norm throughout the history of the institution.

9. It's probably controversial.

Now, here is the first of two school systems we know about as of the writing of the first edition of this book.

The Montessori Schools National

> *"Our aim is not merely to make the child understand,*
> *and still less to force him to memorize,*
> *but so to touch his imagination as to enthuse*
> *him to his inmost core."*
> — Dr. Maria Montessori

The Montessori school system is perhaps the most widely known school of its type. With a lineage that started in Rome with Dr. Montessori's day-care center in 1907, these wonderful schools blossomed into a nationwide system of licensed schools and educators that feature children as "independent learners." The American Montessori Society (AMS) was eventually founded in 1960.

Their unique application of revolutionary teaching methods seems to have been written to match what we have all been describing as necessary for the Indigo Children's education. Here is the basis of their philosophy as published within their own material.

The *whole child* approach is what makes Montessori education unique. The primary goal of a Montessori program is to help each child reach full potential in all areas of life. Activities promote the development of social skills, emotional growth, and physical coordination as well as cognitive preparation. The holistic curriculum, under the direction of a specially prepared teacher, allows the child to experience the joy of learning, time to enjoy the process and ensure the development of self-esteem, and provides the experiences from which children create their knowledge.

Dr. Montessori's developmentally appropriate approach was designed to fit each child instead of making each child fit the program. Respect for each child's individuality is at the core of her philosophy. And this respect leads to the development of trusting relationships.

The Montessori organization also trains teachers. There are now over 3,000 private, publicly funded, and public Montessori schools in America. You'll find them in affluent suburbs, in migrant worker communities, in inner cities, and in rural settings. You'll find them with children from the broadest range of social, cultural, ethnic and economic backgrounds.

Learn more by writing to:

American Montessori Society (AMS)
150 Fifth Avenue
New York, NY 10011
(212) 924-3209

The Waldorf Schools Worldwide

*"Waldorf Schools are in the most impressive way
concerned with quality in education. All schools would do
well to become knowledgeable about the philosophy
that underlies Waldorf education."*
— Dr. Boyer, director of the Carnegie Foundation for Education

The Montessori schools are an established and well-known alternative system. Equally tried and true are the Waldorf Schools, also known as Rudolf Steiner Schools.

In 1919, the first Waldorf school in the world opened in Stuttgart, Germany. The first Waldorf school in North America, the Rudolf Steiner School of New York, opened in 1928. Today it is reported that Waldorf is the largest and fastest-growing nonsectarian educational movement in the world, with 550 schools in over 30 countries. The movement is very strong in western Europe, especially in Germany, Austria, Switzerland, the Netherlands, Great Britain, and the Scandinavian countries. There are approximately 100 schools in North America.

Even back in 1919, the Free Waldorf School's explicit purpose was to create free, creative, independent, moral, happy human beings. Steiner summarized its task: "Accept the children with reverence, educate them with love, send them forth in freedom." Do you think Steiner had any idea about the Indigos? He was indeed a forward-thinking educator! Here is a quote from an article in the *East West Journal,* in 1989, by Ronald E. Kotzsch, Ph.D.:

> Entering a Waldorf school is like passing through Alice's looking glass into an educational Wonderland. It is a surprising, sometimes disorienting world of fairy tales, myths and legends, of music, art, physics demonstrations, class plays and seasonal festivals, of workbooks written and illustrated by stu-

dents, a world without exams, grades, computers or televisions. It is, in short, a world where most of the standard ideas and practices of American Education have been stood on their heads.

Learn more by contacting:

Association of Waldorf Schools of North America
3911 Bannister Rd.
Fair Oaks, CA 95628
(916) 961-0927
www.ch.steiner.school.nz/waldir.html

Other Techniques

Some of the following processes are really profound. They don't fall into the classic category of schooling and education that we have been discussing, but nevertheless they are basic human learning issues. One of the things that amazes me about them is how *intuitive* and *simple* they are. Yet they are often forgotten and must then be brought back to us by men and women of insight. Again, these are offered as only a few of the many processes that doubtless are being used right now with wonderful results. Some may seem weird to you, but we only offer those that we absolutely know are getting results.

Love Training—the Energy of the Heart

Jan and I tour the world as self-help lecturers. We talk about the basis for the most healthy human attitude and spirit—which is *love* of self and of others. Through this awesome natural energetic power, health and peace are achieved, personalities are balanced, and we even live longer! It is our tool, and we teach it everywhere.

Remember the words of Robert Ocker in the last section? He said that the children "will understand, by your ethic of care and intent of compassion, that to share your love with them is to love yourself and celebrate the place where we are all One." Over and over in this book you will read about love. Now let us present a systems researcher who has a practical construct around this very issue!

We read a short article in *Venture Inward*[47] magazine about what **David McArthur** was doing, and our hearts were truly warmed. He has co-authored a book with his late father, Bruce, called *The Intelligent Heart.*[48] Mr. McArthur, an attorney and Unity minister, is director of the Personal Empowerment and Religious Divisions of the Institute of HeartMath in Boulder Creek, California.

The Intelligent Heart expounds with great detail and clarity about how love is the key to all the things we speak of. In addition, Mr. McArthur writes that the heart is our center that effectively manages the distribution of energy through all the centers of our body. Electromagnetic "signatures" of the heart, as measured through electrocardiograms, are presented in the book that dramatically show the attributes of frustration and anger as compared to appreciation and peace. The chaotic patterns of angry emotions (called incoherent spectrums) are profoundly different from the orderly and uniform patterns (the coherent spectrums) of peaceful emotions.

This book is really about love, and how to go from the chaotic pattern to the ordered pattern on demand—a process that, although it is thought to originate in the brain, actually involves your heart, or more accurately, the emotional sensitivities that we call our "heart." The information is practical and wonderfully complete. It is for all humans, not just children. It's a great "how to" for those who love to see practical information about areas of emotion that are often difficult to get control of.

Next, we wish to make you aware of a technique called Freeze-Frame. To honor its practitioners, we will not present it here, because it needs to be taught correctly, within the correct structure, and with all necessary training.

The Freeze-Frame exercise was created by Doc Childre and is a basic technique of the HeartMath system. The Institute of HeartMath has developed several stress-reduction exercises. Freeze-Frame is designed to smooth out the heart rhythm and jump-start those coherent spectrum patterns that we just discussed. We encourage you to contact the HeartMath organization[49] if you are interested in Doc Childre's book, *Freeze-Frame: One Minute Stress Management,*[50] or David McArthur's book, *The Intelligent Heart.*[48]

The Freeze-Frame method was suggested to us by **Pauline Rogers,** who contacted us. She is a credentialed and active worker in child development. She received the Child Development advocacy award from the California Child Development Administrators Association (CCDAA), and has been the recipient of the Sue Brock Fellowship to study advocacy in the field of child development. Her qualifications are quite impressive, showing a lifetime of dedication to children, and she called us to help in any way she could.

We asked Pauline, "What are the best methods you have seen being taught today to help our kids?" She spoke of the Freeze-Frame® method of approaching problems as being a method for everyone, including children. She also spoke of new, noncompetitive games being used in classes.

Pauline uses a slightly modified version of the Freeze-Frame method for young children, since it is simple to understand. She says, "The exercise teaches tolerance, patience, and responsibility for being aware of answers from the heart level. It's a nonconfrontational way to solve problems, and it can be used to make decisions too. I recommend Freeze-Frame highly as a teaching tool and a life tool."

Noncompetitive Life Games
Pauline Rogers

Another way that tolerance can be taught is through noncompetitive games. Such games are found in the wonderful books, *The Incredible Indoor Games Book*[51] and *The Outrageous Outdoor Games Book*.[52] Years ago, we discovered that children learn through games. The invaluable High Scope teaching methods incorporate real-life activities and games to teach children about life and living together. Currently, several schools practice these methods.

Work with Indigo Children absolutely must include all levels of development: physical, mental, emotional, social, and spiritual. Take the "whole child" approach, or else risk the lopsided development that our schools have achieved. Presently, very little social or self-responsibility is being taught or exhibited in our schools. Adults must be role models.

Other books I recommend from Planetary Publications are: *A Parenting Manual, Teen Self Discovery*, and *Teaching Children to Love*—all by Doc Lew Childre[50]; *Meditating with Children*, by Deborah Rozman[53]; *The Ultimate Kid*, by Jeffrey Goelitz[54]; and *Joy in the Classroom*, by Stephanie Herzog.[55]

Ayurvedic Disciplines for Children

Ever heard of Deepak Chopra? He is, perhaps, one of the most well-known names in the self-help field. Among other things, Dr. Chopra teaches the 5,000-year-old "Science of Life" called Ayurveda, a process sweeping the planet in a reawakening of its wise application to everyday life and health.

Joyce Seyburn, a former worker with Dr. Chopra, has taken this science and applied it specifically to children! Her new book, *Seven Secrets to Raising a Healthy and Happy Child: The Mind/Body Approach to Parenting,*[56] guides her readers through yoga, breathing, nutrition, massage, and Ayurvedic concepts designed to nurture the parents, and, in so doing, better prepare them for nurturing the child. Here, Joyce brings you a brief synopsis of this fine new book.

Seven Secrets to Raising a Healthy and Happy Child
Joyce Golden Seyburn

I believe that nurturing your child gives the foundation needed to withstand all the changes, stresses, and challenges that will be coming at them throughout life. Following are seven important ways to nurture your child.

The first secret is to care for your baby in the womb, from the moment of conception. Practice a balanced lifestyle by exercising moderately on a regular basis, eating nutritionally, getting enough rest, and nurturing yourself.

The second secret is to learn your child's mind/body type, or *dosha*. The information on mind/body types was derived from Ayurveda, or the "Science of Life," a 5,000-year-old all-inclusive preventive health system from ancient India. To learn your child's mind/body type, observe their eating and sleeping patterns, sensitivity to light and noise, and interaction with others.

The third secret is to learn the balance between how to center yourself and how to calm and soothe your baby or child. The best way to do this is through some type of meditation, either vocal or silent. Since children don't need to meditate, but they do need ways to center and calm themselves. Another way to achieve this goal is through the senses, using music, walks in nature, aromatherapy, or the like.

The fourth secret is daily body massage, which helps the baby with digestion and resistance to disease, and improves sleep patterns and muscle tone. Massage for older children and adults helps relieve muscle tension and also releases endorphins under the skin, which makes you feel good.

The fifth secret is to introduce yoga and breathing techniques to your baby, as well as to your older children. This lifetime practice will improve alertness and coordination; and regulate hunger, thirst, sleep, and digestion.

The sixth secret is to make the proper nutritional choices to best serve individual mind/body types. When parents establish examples by following the practices mentioned above, the tempo for a life of balance and health will be rooted in their children.

The seventh secret is to use rest, massage, tonics, and diet to ease childbirth, avoid postpartum depression, and nurture your baby and yourself.

By nurturing your child and following these tips, you and your child can enjoy more peaceful and stable lives.

Touch—New Evidence That It Is More Than It Appears

Perhaps you don't want to rush out and "buy into" a 5,000-year-old health system. Well, if you wait long enough, it will come to you! Joyce Seyburn's fourth secret, above, is now mainstream.

In a July 1998 *Time* magazine article entitled "Touch Early and Often," Tammerlin Drummond[57] gives us the following information:

> Studies at the Touch Research Institute have found that preemies massaged three times a day for as few as five days consistently fare better than equally frail babies who don't get massages. Full term infants and older babies also benefit from them.

The same article quotes Dr. Tiffany Field, the Miami child psychologist who founded the Touch Research Institute six years ago. She says that massage stimulates the vagus nerves, which then trigger processes that aid digestion, among other things. As a result of their speedy weight gain, Field says, massaged preemies are discharged to their parents an average of six days earlier, shaving $10,000 off their hospital tab. With 400,000 premature babies born in the U.S. every year, the potential savings are apparent. And eight months after birth, Field says, massaged preemies have superior motor skills and mental development. In chapter 4, be ready for some alternate methods of healing and balance, as well as some day-to-day regimens that you may never have thought existed. Again, we include them because they're *working*.

More Warm and Fuzzy Stories about the Indigos

Once again, we will conclude with true stories about these special Indigo Children. The following stories illustrate the substance and inner meaning of the Indigo phenomenon. Meet some more of the new kids!

My daughter asked for some cough medicine the other day. When I hesitated to give her any, she told me, "You know, Mom, it's not really the medicine that's helping me . . . . it's just that I believe it will work, so it does!"

Another time, I was sitting next to the mother of a three-year-old while waiting for my daughter at horseback-riding lessons. The woman told me that her daughter was driving her nuts, constantly asking questions that she couldn't answer, and the daughter would become very frustrated. She told her mom, "You are supposed to know all the answers! It's in the rules!"

"What rules?" her mom asked.

*"The mommy rules. You are supposed to tell all the answers!"
the child insisted.*

*When Mom again replied that she just didn't have all the
answers, the daughter impatiently stomped her foot. "I do not like
this, being a child!" she said. "I want to be the grown-up NOW!"*

*Later that week, the daughter was very angry at her dad for
placing some restrictions on her. She angrily told him, "You have
to be nice to me! You wanted me, so you had me. Now you'd better take care of me!"*

— Linda Etheridge, teacher

*My wife and I tell Nicholas, age two, that we love him.
Sometimes he'll tell us that he loves us back, but more often than
not, Nicholas will agree with us: "I love me, too."*

— John Owen, dad

*Once my angels told me that the stars were angels, too, and
their names were the Star Angels. They told me that every star was
somebody's angel here on Earth. And the wishing star was everybody's angel. And the Star Angels were meant to look after everybody here on Earth no matter what.*

— Megan Shubick, age 8

chapter three

Spiritual Aspects of Indigos

P lease note: If you are at all offended by New Age metaphysics or spiritual talk in general, then please skip this chapter. We don't want the information contained here to bias your feelings about this book, or the principles being presented in the other chapters.

For some, this subject is foolishness and goes against common spiritual teachings in the Western world. The perception might be that it contains information that goes against doctrinal issues taught from birth about God and established religion. Therefore, it might cause you to question your acceptance of the quality information coming in subsequent chapters.

Yet for others, it is the Holy Grail of the whole message!

We are just going to report what we have seen and heard. We have no interest whatsoever in swaying you toward any spiritual philosophy. If you have noted a bias in the writing, it's there—but it's about *love*, and the treatment of the new children—not about religion or philosophy.

If you doubt metaphysics, please go on to chapter 4, where we get into health, especially ADD and ADHD. Skipping this chapter completely won't change our core message about the Indigo Children.

For the Rest of You

This chapter contains a collection of stories from all over the world, and even a prophecy that targets the Indigo Children as "those who know where they came from, and who they used to be."

Television personality Gordon Michael Scallion (*Prophecies and Predictions*) predicted the arrival of the new "dark blue children," and there are other spiritual historians who point to similar predictions in ancient texts.

Is reincarnation—"life before life"—real? Are the countless stories of children telling their parents who they "used to be" a common fantasy of a rich, intelligent mind—or a deep remembrance that we should look at?

What do you tell your children when they say they were here before, or when they tell you about the "angel friends" or other spiritual aspects that were not learned from any source you were responsible for? What about when they begin correcting your religious doctrine? What do you do then?

We wish we had the answers to all these questions. We can tell you that you should *never* belittle children for relaying this information. If it goes against your belief system, then simply ignore it. However, we personally would be grabbing our pencils! These "messages" will sort themselves out over time and may not affect later religious teaching. Most children forget these episodes after they are about seven. Regarding religion, we have strong evidence that kids can hardly wait for church! This spiritual overlay is a brand-new attribute of human children, and it's worth reporting—all of it.

Before we start, let's define a couple of terms that will be used in this chapter:

- **Past life:** The idea that the human soul is eternal, and that an eternal soul participates in more than one human life over time.

- **Karma:** The energy of a past life or series of past lives, believed to help shape the potentials of learning and personality traits in the current life.

- **Aura:** Life force around a person, sometimes "seen" intuitively with various colors that have meaning.

- **Vibration:** Also referred to as "frequency." *High vibration* is a term used to describe an enlightened state of being.

- **Old energy:** The old ways, often describing an unenlightened state.

- **Lightworker:** A person in a high vibration who is enlightened and doing high spiritual work. Normally used to describe a layperson.

- **Reiki:** A system of energy balance.

Jan and I greatly respect the following scholar. Her work in homeopathy has impressed us, and even balanced us a few times. **Melanie Melvin, Ph.D., DHM, RSHom,** is a world-class counselor and Fellow of the British Institute for Homeopathy. Find her on the Internet at: **www.drmelanie.com.** Her contribution covers many subjects, but Melanie always considers her work firmly anchored and melded to the spiritual.

Respecting the Indigo Children
Melanie Melvin, Ph.D.

Indigos come into this life with self-respect and an unshakable understanding that they are children of God. Your Indigo will be quite confused and dismayed if you do not have the same knowledge that you, too, are a spiritual being above all else. Therefore, it is crucial that you respect yourself. Nothing turns an Indigo off faster than parents who do not earn their child's respect, but who instead give away their power and parental responsibility to the child.

When our son, Scott, was two and a half years old, he ran into the kitchen, heading for the wet floor I had just washed. Still down on my knees, I stretched out my arm to prevent him from falling and sliding across the wet floor. He raised himself to his full stature, looked me squarely in the eyes, and with great power and determination said, "Don't push Scottie." He perceived that he had been disrespected and was standing up for himself. I was impressed at the indomitable spirit in that little body!

You cannot fake this technique with your children. Your self-respect must come from inside. If you are simply trying to follow the recommended techniques of some "expert," these children will sense it. You must be sincere and be who you truly are—all you can be. You must be a role model for your children. Children learn mostly from modeling their parents' example, not from words. If these children feel that their parents' example does not have integrity, they will turn away. In any case, they will not completely imitate their parents, because they clearly have their own identity.

One example of a mother trying to "fake a technique" with her daughter occurred when her daughter was playing with mine. The mother came to pick up her very independent, self-willed three-year-old. She was trying to be very nice and repeatedly told her daughter that it was time to leave. Yet she was giving all her power to her daughter, who felt only disdain for her mother's weakness.

As this went on, the mother became more frustrated and angry, yet kept speaking sweetly and pleadingly to the little girl. Finally, when I couldn't stand it any longer, I said to the girl, "If you don't go home when your mother wants you to, she will not want to bring you the next time you want to visit." The little one looked at me, understood, and left with her mom.

If Mom had been honest and come from a position of respect and strength, she would have simply said, "I need to go home, what do you need to do to get ready to leave?" The situation would then have proceeded more smoothly. When Indigos feel you are dealing with them with integrity and respect for them as people with rights, they are more willing to cooperate and deal honestly with you. If they sense manipulation and guilt, it raises their dander.

Respect yourself, respect your children as other spiritual beings, and expect respect from them in turn. While watching other children speak to their parents disrespectfully, my children said to me, "Mommy, you would never let us get away with that!" and they respected and appreciated me for this. One of the most common mistakes I see in modern parents is bending over backwards to never "hurt or damage" their child psychologically. What about the damage done by giving free reign to your children in a world that is too big for them to handle without their parents' leadership?

See your children as equal to you spiritually, but also as aware that you are the parent this time and therefore the one in the position of responsibility. They are not in charge, but they are honored. They are given every choice and freedom that they are capable of handling. For example, they are allowed to choose what they would like to eat out of what you may have prepared for a meal, or they may help you choose what you fix for a meal. Yet, you are not a short-order cook, fixing something different for everyone. I have seen mothers run ragged trying to please everyone in this way. This is disrespectful to those mothers. If one member of the family is sacrificed, the other members cannot benefit. The family situation must support every member.

The angriest children I have seen in my role as a psychologist and homeopath are those without parental limits. I have witnessed children push their parents to anger just so the parents would set limits on the children's behavior. You are abdicating your role as a parent if you allow your child to control you.

When our son was two, I told him not to touch something on the coffee table. He touched it just to test me. I knew it was a test and smacked his fingers. He touched it again and again and again, and got his finger smacked each time. He was in tears, and my heart was breaking, but I knew that if I gave in he would be more deeply harmed. It would mean that he had beaten the parent, who was supposed to be bigger, stronger, more dependable, and able to keep him safe—*and that is frightening for a child!* After that incident, we hugged; he was happy and never needed to go to that extreme again. If I had given in, we would have had to repeat that scenario many, many times until learning the lesson to be strong, not overly sympathetic, and aware of the bigger picture.

When there is a pattern of defiance in an Indigo Child, it is usually because they feel disrespected or feel that you are not respecting yourself by giving your power away to them. Periodically, any child may test your authority. Respect yourself and your child, and you won't go wrong. Respect is based in love. If you truly love your children and are not looking to them to fill your needs to be loved and accepted, the highest good for all concerned will be served.

Freedom of Choice

Freedom is very important to Indigo Children. True freedom is accompanied by responsibility for the choices made. These choices must be appropriate to the maturity of the child. For example, as a preteen, our daughter Heather was invited to go to Disneyland with her friend's family. However, she had a cold and her friend's parents would be smoking in the car, which always made Heather sick. Also, she had just gone to Disneyland and wasn't sure she wanted to spend the money again so soon. Yet it's hard for any kid to say no to Disneyland, and she didn't want to let her friend down.

She was confused, overwhelmed with the decision, and didn't feel well. I knew this was too great a test for her level of wisdom, and she really wanted to stay home but couldn't say no. So I told her she needed to stay home. She cried from disappointment, but then felt relieved and later thanked me for not letting her go.

Similarly, at 18, Heather had recovered from a viral infection just in time to go to her senior prom on a Saturday night, returning home early Sunday morning. Sunday night, she was supposed to drive herself and her friends about an hour from home to go dancing. She was having second thoughts about going because the weekend was so packed with activities. She knew she might suffer a relapse, but the fun she anticipated having was worth it. I told her she was free to stay home if she wished, and she stated firmly that she was going, so I respected her decision.

In both cases, I respected her underlying desires, stepped in when I felt she needed help, and stood back when she made a firm decision. Respect and discernment were required in both cases. Heather gained experience in both situations. Since being alive is all about gaining experience, there are no wrong choices, since we acquire wisdom no matter what we choose. As parents we need to guide, educate, and encourage, but allow natural and logical consequences to teach our children as often as possible. Indigos, especially, will become defiant if they feel that another's will is being imposed on them.

Indigos already feel that they are different from others. The labels of hyperactivity and ADHD make them believe that they are different in a bad way. This leads to discouragement, depression, and a vicious cycle of negative behavior and moods, which robs them of their potential and gifts.

There is emotional pain behind their inability to sit still or concentrate. When they are treated as if they are bad, they initially become angry at the devaluing of their self-worth. However, like brainwashing, overwhelming devaluation eventually sinks in. One such Indigo was an angelic-looking blue-eyed blonde. She was a new four-year-old at the Montessori school. She had screaming temper tantrums that prompted neighbors of the school to call and see what the teachers were doing to that poor child! Yet, it was "Angel" who was kicking teachers and bullying other kids, while watching her own performance in the mirror with great satisfaction!

This little girl was angry with her mother for not respecting her and giving her freedom. She was angry with her teachers for allowing her too much freedom to abuse others. This little Indigo was not too impressed with the adults in her life. She felt more capable and smarter on one level, yet put down on another—so she set out to prove who was better! She was secretly hoping someone would rise to the occasion.

It is always easier for an outside professional who is not so emotionally involved to retain detachment and perspective. So during our sessions, the first thing I did was establish who was in charge. I was firm, loving, fair, and respectful, and expected the same from her. The second thing I did was give her a homeopathic remedy. This makes my job as a psychologist a lot easier. The remedy stimulates the cells of the body to rebalance disharmony. The day after the remedy was given, the teachers called to see what happened because a miracle had occurred. Angel was being an angel—no tantrums, no kicking, no bullying!

However, I knew the job was not complete. We had to work with the adults now that Angel had become more balanced; otherwise, the environment would throw her out of harmony again, and she would not respond so readily next time. She needed her mother and teachers to be strong, firm, and loving so that she could trust them and feel secure enough to settle down to do her work. We all need a feeling of basic security before we can go on to fulfill our purpose.

As her anger mollified, the underlying hurt surfaced—she felt disliked by the other kids and different in a bad way.

Another homeopathic remedy for grief and loss along with some counseling helped heal the emotional wounds. We also focused on her learning some social skills.

We would not want the Indigos to be like everyone else, but it is a difficult road to be different. They sometimes feel lonely and not a part of the group—that hurts. However, it doesn't help to tell them that they are not different; they know they are. Instead, help them to see that the difference is valuable. Ask them if they would like to be just like everyone else, citing specific examples; they are likely to say no. This reminds them of their choice to be who they are.

The Independent Indigos

Generally, Indigos are independent beings. So when they go their own way, don't take it personally. Their intensity of purpose is admirable, but it can also feel like a freight train heading for you!

My husband and I saw a mother and little girl in a restaurant. The mother expected her daughter to idly wait while the mother ate breakfast. Mom must have been thinking of her own childhood when children were expected to be seen and not heard. It's a child's nature to be busy; they have a lot to learn. With the Indigo this is magnified; they have a strong sense of purpose.

This little girl, probably three years old, had been seated on a wooden high chair with no protective tray, since the chair was to be pulled up to the table. However, the chair was too high for the table where Mom was sitting, so she left it about a foot away so that her daughter couldn't crawl up on the table. Mom told us that she expected her to sit there because she had been told to. However, my husband, Sid, and I had observed this child for a minute or two, looked at each other, and simultaneously said, "Indigo."

We had observed the intense and totally matter-of-fact look in the child's eyes, and how she felt equal to the adults in the room. She was not shy or fearful, or even concerned about whether we approved of her. She was standing on the high chair.

She was not standing up to defy her mother; she had no sense that she was doing something wrong. She was standing from some internal motivation. Even though she was standing at a height, I had no fear that she might fall, nor did she; her balance was perfect. She had total confidence in herself and inspired confidence in us.

It was her mother that I was concerned about. If she expected to deal with this child with outmoded ideas, she would have her hands full. I empathetically said to her mother, "She knows her own mind!" hoping to imply that that's a good trait. Her mom responded, "She sure does!" with mixed exasperation and pride.

The child heard all that we were saying, took it in stride, and continued to self-reference—to make her own choices, following her own internal intuition, values, motivation, and discernment. Had Mom given her daughter something to do and communicated her concerns about the potential for falling, they probably would have reached a compromise and both been happier.

As long as the Indigo's self-referencing independence is tempered with concern for others, it is an advantage not to instill in her the guilt, fear of others' opinions, and lack of trust in her own intuition that previous generations have had to face.

They Are What They Eat

Here is another area where the new kids do not have our legacy. Eating is not such a big deal with them. They don't tend to consume large amounts of food—quite a concern to many parents. Yet this is ironic, considering how uptight most of us are about our weight! They will eat what they need to sustain their bodies; they will not starve.

Their livers can also metabolize more junk food than we can, although many of them seem to prefer living food such as vegetables and fruits, as well as meats and fish. They tend to eat smaller amounts and don't worry about their next meal. These children do not respond to guilt, trickery, fear, or manipulation, so if you resort to such techniques, you will only lose their respect. If you are concerned or have some nutritional information to offer, share it with them. Then back off and let them make their own choices. Their body's wisdom will tell them what they need much more clearly if they are not contaminated with fads and fears, shoulds and shouldn'ts.

An experiment was done in the 1970s with a large number of children two and a half years and under. They were presented with a large buffet of foods each time they ate. They were allowed to choose whatever they liked with no admonitions. Contrary to what the researchers expected, the children chose a variety of nutritious foods and did not overdo sweets. One child with rickets drank cod liver oil until the rickets were cured. If kids in the mid-'70s did this, why not trust the Indigos to choose what their bodies need?

From the Heart

These children have a compassion for other living things: the planet, life in general, animals, plant life, and other people. They react to cruelty, unfairness, inhumanity, stupidity, callousness, and insensitivity. Although they want things, they have a lack of materialism (unless they are overindulged) and are usually generous.

Research in the field of psychology consistently indicates that parents who are sensitive and reach out to help their children, in turn have children who are sensitive and reach out to others. Recent findings showed that when someone was helping another, the helper's heart rate went down. Those who tend to be nonhelpers have higher heart rates. In addition, the helpers (not co-dependents!) helped even when they could have left the scene. They helped because it came from their hearts.

To put it simply, the children who were empathetic also tended to be assertive and have lower heart rates. They were emotionally, mentally, socially, and physically more healthy. Those with the least altruism were typically the most miserable with their lives. The empathetic children were also relatively assertive and were not seen by others as easy targets for excessive requests for help.

Research also indicates that high morals come from empathy. Empathy is learned by being treated with compassion. Respect your kids' inherent ability to survive and fulfill their potential. They have come in with particular problems and abilities for the experience. Don't fret over what they've chosen. Rather, trust in the wisdom of the plan, and offer some guidance and support along the way. Be yourself, and admit problems and mistakes; then, they will feel free to do the same. Be honest about your emotions. Let them know you love them.

Helping others not only comes from the heart, but is good for the heart. We have concrete evidence that altruism is healthy emotionally and physically! Even before the advent of any ability to verbalize moral principles or conceptualize them, children will show empathy.

My son, Scott, showed this at the age of 17 months. Feeling sick and at the end of my endurance, I started to cry. When Scottie saw my tears, I tried to walk away, but he asked about my crying, so I told him I was upset. He asked to be lifted up and then proceeded to point to pictures on the walls, and toys that I might be interested in. This is exactly what I would do to help him change his focus when he was upset. He was doing for me what I had done for him, and it worked!

On another occasion when Heather wanted my attention, I said to her, "You can't have Mommy right now." Scottie was nearby and said with emphasis, "But she needs you!" He was under three years old, and Heather was about eight months. Even very small children can read emotional needs in another.

Moral development is born of compassion. A code of ethics comes from the heart, not from a rigid set of rules. In a crisis, it is the heart, not the head, that rules. Bravery and courage result from a habitual feeling of unselfishness and a willingness to risk oneself for the benefit of another, not from logically thinking through the pros and cons of the situation.

In the end, it is not our thinking that determines whether we do the right thing, but our hearts.

Strong Will, Strong Soul

These children are wholly determined to get what they want. The tough part is when they badger you until they get what they want! You are better off saying, "Let me think about it," rather than saying no right off the bat. They generally have good reasons for what they want, which may cause you to reconsider your answer and then back down.

It's better to hear out their reasons and then consider carefully before answering. If you say no and then relent, they will quickly learn to keep pestering until they get their way. This does not mean you should give them everything they want, but rather, mean what you say when you answer yes or no to their request.

A Sense of Responsibility

The primary rule is to have fewer rules, and more guidelines and principles of behavior. If Indigos have values and principles, they can think through the best course of action. Help them develop a code of ethics from the heart. When you are not there, their interactions and decisions will come from a place of love, as opposed to depending on an authority figure to tell them what to do, or waiting until the authority figure leaves to do exactly what they want.

Most humans do not respond well to orders. Better to be a loving and trusted confidant and counselor than to be only a disciplinarian. Define boundaries before you enforce them. Gear demands to the level of the child, allow for childish irresponsibility, and allow natural and logical consequences to teach your child. Discuss issues with your children, and allow them to have a say. Trust them, and they are likely to be trustworthy.

Love Is the Key

Remember that this child of yours has had as many (more or less) lifetimes as you, and therefore is a spiritual being just as you are, with particular experiences, talents, karma, and character traits. Your children incarnated to be with you. They picked you as parents to learn certain lessons, gain experience, develop certain aspects of their character, and work on strengthening their weaker areas of spiritual development.

This does not absolve you of your responsibilities as a parent, but it does absolve you of being totally accountable for whatever your children become. As spiritual beings, they are equal to you. They have chosen to be your kids this time; perhaps you were their children in some other lifetime. You know how parents often say, "Just wait until you have kids. I hope they are just like you!" Well, perhaps that is why your kids are your kids this time! We are more like our kids, and they are more like us, than we care to admit.

The greatest opportunity we have for growth is in our relationships with others. It is only as we see ourselves reflected in them that we get feedback on who we are. If you can see the issues your children bring up for you as opportunities for character development for both you and them, you will find the problems much less troublesome. We only add to the difficulties when we worry, blame, or try to escape the challenges we are facing with our kids. Look at what is tough for you to handle in your kids; then see what the lesson is for you. As you deal with this, you will release the struggle with the child, and your relationship will improve. Remember to see the humor in the situation or relationship, and feel the love you have for this human who is very special to you.

Feel honored, because they chose you for a reason, and rise to the task at hand. Give them your time, your attention, and yourself; this is love. Kids remember the important events with you, but they don't remember how often they occurred. So give fully to them whenever you can.

Now, **Robert Ocker** returns to these pages. As an educator and a "heart specialist," he has more information.

A Heart-Centered Journey
Robert P. Ocker

Working with a support group of middle-school kids on anger management, I asked the group to write down a significant experience in their lives. The group then shared their responses verbally. It was my intent, as the facilitator, to help the children focus on self-esteem.

An eighth-grade boy stood up in confidence and asked, "Do you know what the most significant experience in the last 100 years was?" The group looked at each other, then at me, and said no. This Indigo kid replied with sincere intent, "Me!"

The other kids in the group started to laugh, as middle-school kids do when they are uncomfortable or do not understand. I sensed the energy in the room changing to a lower vibration. I gently and respectfully approached this gift of a person and looked into his confused eyes with wisdom. I said, with the intent of honor and respect, "That you are! I am glad you are here. We are grateful for your guidance; you have taught the group that laughter and peace overcome anger. Thank you!"

The Indigo kid returned the smile in my eyes with his warm smile and laughed. Again the energy changed in the room. This time it was an energy of peace.

The confidence of Indigos is a major factor in determining their future success. The preservation of a child's native esteem is far more important than the acquisition of technical skills. Share with them the knowledge they need, but preserve their inherent confidence in themselves, for this is how they show their confidence in God.

As Ken Carey states in his book *The Third Millennium:*

> Many of these Little Ones have not forgotten the Great Being who shines through the filter of their individuality. Your role is to help them grow in such a way that they do not forget. Assist the incarnation of the eternal spirits who dance above their lives.
>
> When you see first their beauty and perfection, when you affirm their eternal reality of being, when you see it in their eyes, you cannot help but draw it forth. Bring out the best in them and in all whom you encounter. Give no energy to the fictions of those who do not know their immortality, but see instead the spirit who seeks to incarnate there, within that individuality. Acknowledge that Being. Relate to it. Draw it forth. Help another dimension of eternity slip quietly into your times. Help this new generation to awaken.

The Power of Play: Gateway to the Universe

"You can discover more about a person in an hour of play than in a year of conversation."
— Plato

I tried to reach the child from words;
they passed him by often unheard.

I tried to reach the child from books;
he gave me only puzzled looks.

Despairingly, I turned aside.
"How should I reach this child?" I cried.

Into my ear he whispered.
"Come," he said, "Play with me!"
— Writer unknown

When we play with the Little Ones, the angels play with the stars. The power of play opens up the playgates of the universe where we all play with the Creator—a joyous play, a game of love, giving and receiving. Honor and learn from the Little Ones' intent to play. They will teach us the innocence in their hearts that embrace unconditional love. They shall inherit the earth with this love.

Within the children's minds and hearts are their imaginations and visions of planet Earth. This is the Indigo's mission: to prepare humanity for the universal song of love. These visions will inspire the universe to one song. Hear these visions. See their hope and guide it, for this is the vision of tomorrow in the imaginations of today.

Feel the playfulness of these imaginations. It is in this energy that we can find free choice, which will quicken the universe. It is this energy that will play for us the song of the stars and the song of the universe. Hear the imaginations of the Little Ones. Listen, and inspire them. The Little Ones are losing their ability to dream of a universe within their hearts. Understand their intentions, and lead them to make choices that will help the planet grow toward peace. It is peace that they know. Through peace they are teaching us a greater understanding of humanity.

Laugh with the Little Ones

Laughter is the key! Listen to the laughter of the Little Ones; as they laugh, the stars radiate with joy. For their laughter is joy and hope for the new light shining on planet Earth—the planet of free choice, the planet of laughter. Are not our children too serious? What about the elders? Are they not teaching the Little Ones by their examples? Laugh with this, and understand that the Little Ones need to, as well. Their hearts demand it. The stars demand it. The universe demands it. Laughter is necessary for the planet to continue to vibrate with love, joy, and peace. Laugh with the Little Ones!

Here is the final installment of Jan's interview with **Nancy Tappe.**

Indigo Spirituality
Nancy Ann Tappe, interviewed
by Jan Tober (Part III)

Nancy, are any of these Indigos here for the first time?

Yes, some are. There are some who have already gone through the third dimension, and there are some, I think, who came from another planet. That's the *inter-planets* Indigo—why I call them *interdimensional.* But the Artist, Conceptual, and Humanist types [see chapter 1] have all been here and gone through the color system.

Do they come in with karma?

Yes, they can come in with karma. They are not karmi-cally free. If you watch the Indigos between birth and age two, they remember other lifetimes.

That's another story I love to tell. I have stories three miles long about my grandson, Colin. One day I came home from work when my daughter Laura and he were there, because they lived with me the first five years of his life.

And she said to me, "Oh, Mom, you're gonna love this. Let Colin tell you what he told me today." And Colin said, "Nah, I don't want to tell. I don't want to tell." Laura said, "Go ahead and tell Mano; she loves these stories." And very fast, he said, "I was just telling Mom when we lived in Land Magog, and she was not my mother then—she was my friend and history came along and we weren't anymore." And I said, "That's interesting." He looked at me and laughed and said, "You know, I just made it up." I said, "Yeah, I know. We all make up things from time to time." Now, where would a child at the age of two get the name *Magog?*

And I have noticed through the years that a lot of Indigos at that young age will talk about other times. I had clients in Laguna Beach, California, who had been students of mine for several years. One day they called me and said, "Nancy, we have a big problem. Can we come in and talk to you?" I said, "Sure, come on in." I took my lunch hour and made room for them.

Their problem was that their two-year-old daughter, three days prior to this, had awakened in the morning and informed them that she was pregnant and had to get back to New York! She told them that she had a daughter in day care and that she was an actress on stage. So I went into my psychic self and tracked her. I said, "You know, as far as I can see, she was indeed an actress on stage, and the theater caught on fire. As everybody was trying to get out, she tripped, and a boulder fell on her; she was trapped. When the firemen came in, she was not burned to death, but she drowned because they turned the hose on without knowing she was there. She drowned." She'd had recall and been crying ever since—going into hysterics, saying they "had to take her to New York."

For three days she was doing this, and my clients said they needed to talk to me because they didn't know what else to do. I told them, "Well, what you must do is just simply go home, sit her down, and tell her, 'Now Melanie, listen: you're looking at another lifetime. Your daughter is older than you are and somebody else is taking care of her. You are not pregnant and you do not belong in New York. You are looking at another lifetime.' Talk to her as if she were an adult." They did, and later told me, "You know, we haven't heard a word from her since. She has never mentioned it to this day."

Indigo Stories

Our son brought his pregnant girlfriend home to live with us. They were briefly married, but separated when still teenagers. She moved away and planned to give the baby away. This was probably the hardest time of my life. Our firstborn grandchild was going to be raised by someone else! Fortunately, they had a change of heart and got back together.

One morning, about six weeks before the baby was due, I got up and began my regular morning routine before work. I noticed a pillar of bright light in the corner of our living room. Shocked, I watched it for a while, then it seemed to fade. I figured it was just the sun or something. The next day it was there again. This time I closed all the curtains and it was still there! I told my husband about it when he came in to have breakfast; he didn't really believe me.

The pillar of light appeared to me every morning for a week. I told everyone in the house about it, but no one believed me.

Monday morning, a week from the first time I saw the light, it appeared again. This time, my husband was walking out of the bedroom, and he saw it. We were both dumbfounded. I had an inner certainty that it was an angel sent to us in preparation for the baby. The light continued to appear until the baby was born and I continued to see it for a couple months after the baby came.

I knew when she was born that she was special, but I wasn't aware of just how special! When I held her, I could sense a familiarity—not just because she was my granddaughter, but as if I had been with her before. At times, it seemed she was holding me, not the other way around. When she was about three months old, she would lift her arms to the ceiling, and I'd ask her if she could see the angel. I know this sounds strange, but I could almost see the "yes" in her little brown eyes.

As time went on, it was apparent that we had a special child on our hands. She had her own agenda, no matter what, and she's always had the most erratic sleeping habits. She does not like to fall asleep. She told me, when she was around 18 months old, that she didn't like to dream.

When she was two, she found some of my old dolls from when I was a kid. She would stand the biggest one up and call her "Olive." For a two-year-old to say the word Olive *is impressive enough, but even more so when you realize that my mother's name was Olive, and we really never talked that much about my mom around her. Mom passed over two years before Jasmine was born.*

Also, she often says things like, "Way to go, Ed." My father's name was Ed. My parents were together for 42 years before my father passed over.

Jasmine needs to be given at least three choices for anything major. She will not let us read to her, except Goodnight Moon. *She would rather play by herself, watch children's movies, play in the dirt, throw kisses at the moon, hug the trees, and give what she calls "Baby Reiki" to people who are hurt.*

She remembers the blood in her mother's tummy when she lived there before she was born. She says the blood hurt her, and she didn't want to be there. She accepts the fact that her parents don't live together, and loves them both and the people they have in their lives. She loves all children and is a true peacemaker. Her name is Jasmine Brooke VanEtta, and she is three and a half years old.

— Mary and Bill VanEtta

I am the father of Nicholas, age two, who is Indigo. Since his birth, my wife Laura's thyroid gland had become enlarged. She was asked on a Wednesday to undergo a biopsy, which was hurriedly scheduled for that Friday.

In the midst of this, I studied the Dubro EMF Balancing program [see chapter 5]. Discovering and working with this energy that surrounds each and every one of us was a wonderful experience. I thought this would be a great opportunity to put this energy to good use. While praying for my wife's healing, I envisioned a healing green necklace (appropriate since my wife is a retail jeweler) around Laura's thyroid, and continued to give it energy throughout the week while we awaited Laura's results. I'm not particularly sensitive to this energy, and I certainly was never able to see it, but I trusted that it was there and that it would work.

One week after Laura received the initial call to come in for a biopsy, we were at the breakfast table when Nicholas pointed to my wife's face and said "green." Could this child see the energy? My chin hit the floor. I had never mentioned my experiment to

*anyone, much less my two-year-old! I certainly had not men-
tioned anything to my wife. She considers my interest in metaphysical matters rather woo-woo.*

*My wife, of course, immediately assumed that Nicholas was
pointing to her nose, and went for the tissue box. Upon further
inspection, she found nothing. Nicholas repeated, "Mommy, your
face is green." I can only assume that Nicholas was able to see
the green energy necklace that I had created for Laura. It was
there! Was it working? Needless to say, I took it to be a good sign.*

*Later that same morning, Laura received the call from her
doctor that we had been waiting for. The biopsy results were in,
and they were negative. It was nothing.*

— John Owen, father of Nicholas, age two

*I had dreamt that it was possible for me to attract paper to my
hand, as if my hand were magnetized. The dream was so vivid that
I found myself trying to turn the page of a book without touching
it. Aja saw me and asked what I was doing. I said, "Nothing," and
she said, "Are you trying to turn the page without touching it?" I
replied that I was, and she said, "What you need to do is close
your eyes, love God, and see the thing done. It'll be done." Then
she asked me to try, and like the child that she is, she turned the
page while I had my eyes closed.*

— Cheryl Royle, mother of Aja Royle, age six

Matthew fits the description of an Indigo Child perfectly. When he visited me last Christmas, I treated him to a massage by my intuitive healer, Mrs. Bobbi Harris. Not only did he say that he saw "lights moving overhead" in the dimly lit room, but he also said, "Sometimes electricity goes through my brain twice." He has spoken of wanting to go back to God, and even of cremation.

— Sunny Greenberg, grandmother of Matthew, age seven

Some of **Dr. Doreen Virtue's** most recent books are called *The Lightworker's Way, Angel Therapy,* and *Divine Guidance.* As you can see from these titles, she is a spiritual leader. What she really brings to the table, however, is a wonderful meld between real-world practical information and spirituality. What follows is the heart of her message to us. Although chapter 4 will have more from Dr. Virtue about ADD and ADHD, it's important to get her views on how the spiritual aspects of Indigos are related to this diagnosis, so they are presented here as well.

Parenting an Indigo Child
Doreen Virtue, Ph.D.

My views about children stem from a very eclectic background. I'm the mother of two teenaged sons, a psychologist, and the former director of an adolescent chemical dependency program. I'm also a lifelong student of metaphysics and a clairvoyant healer who works with the angelic realm. And, like you, I'm a former child who remembers the emotional issues of growing up.

Do you remember, from your childhood, feeling like an

adult within a small person's body? Practically everyone remembers feeling old or grown-up as a child. I believe this stems from the reincarnation cycle. We are all old souls, yet unless we enter as a walk-in, we must begin each current lifetime as a child.

Still, adults often treat children as if they were . . . well, children. They forget that when they talk to a child, it's no different from talking to an adult. Children expect and deserve the same respect and attention that we accord adults.

It's no coincidence that, in this era preceding the millennium shift, the number of diagnoses for ADHD or ADD have skyrocketed. The number of youths taking Ritalin (methylphenidate) for ADHD has more than doubled between 1990 and 1995, according to a 1996 study by John Hopkins University Medical School.

The Drug Enforcement Administration (DEA) reports that prescriptions for the drug are up 600 percent this decade. According to the DEA, Ritalin is so popular that in some schools, 20 percent of the students are medicated. Journalist John Lang calls them "Generation Rx," adding the ominous statistic that, if the current rate of increase for prescription use continues, by the year 2000 some eight million American schoolchildren will be on the drug.

The trouble is, Ritalin improves behavior at school, but not at home, according to one major study. It's also considered so insidious that the military rejects potential recruits if they have a history of taking Ritalin after age 12. Clearly, drugs aren't the answer.

This increase in childhood psychotropic medication reflects our worldwide discomfort with change. We are on the threshold of leaving behind the old world—based on competition, jealousy, and greed—and entering a new age founded on cooperation, love, and knowledge of our oneness. The old energy is giving way to the new energy.

It seems that everyone, even the most spiritually dense individuals, are aware of these changes. In my spiritual counseling practice, I'm now receiving inquiry calls from, and appointments with, three-piece-suited businessmen. These men want to know, "What's going on?" and "How can I live a more meaningful life?" A few years ago, these men would have never gone near anything reminiscent of psychic phenomena. Now, they are ready to look within for answers, after learning that the corporate world and material acquisitions do not make them feel happy or safe.

Yet, even as the populace embraces—or at least explores—the coming changes, we are still collectively hanging on to old attachments. That is, we resist doing things differently. For example, we still judge, compete, and believe in lack and limitation. And we aren't completely honest with ourselves or others, often hiding behind politeness or political correctness.

The children who have recently incarnated are different from previous generations. They are called "Children of the Light," "Millennium Children," and "Indigo Children" for good reason. These children are highly aware, sensitive, and downright psychic. They also have zero tolerance for dishonesty and inauthenticity. They know when someone is lying, instantly!

So imagine how difficult it is for these children to be in the current educational system, which has much inauthenticity—such as, "Let's pretend that we like being here. Let's not discuss how unhappy we all are to be forced to come to this place and learn/teach things that we're unsure have practical applications in real life."

At home, adults often treat their children dishonestly. For instance, parents may hide things from their children ranging from their true feelings to their drinking habits. Yet these intuitive children know when something is wrong. They may ask Mom or Dad for confirmation of these feelings. If the parents deny the truth, it can drive the children insane with frustration. Children don't know how to reconcile the disparity between what they feel inside (the truth) and what adults are telling them (untruths).

The Indigo Children have incarnated at this time for a very sacred reason: to usher in a new society based on honesty, cooperation, and love. By the time they reach adulthood, our world will be vastly different than it is today. We will no longer have violence and competition. We will remember our ability to manifest our needs, so there will be no need to compete with others. Since our natural telepathic skills will be rekindled, lying will be impossible. And because everyone will realize the oneness that exists between all living beings, thoughtfulness will be the basis of society.

We incur great karmic debt by interfering with children's Divine mission. It is of utmost importance that we help to groom these children for spiritual success. To do so, we must be very honest with them. When children ask about something, even if it makes you uncomfortable, tell them the truth. I often pray for guidance when talking with my own children, so I can speak the truth in a loving way. If you are uncomfortable speaking the truth to children, let them know this. You don't need to turn children into confidantes, but it's important to honestly share your feelings with them. This way, you become a positive role model who shows children how to honor their emotions.

Spiritually Healing Your Parent-Child Relationship

Behind each parent's request to me, "What shall I do about my child?" is an underlying statement that says, "I want my child to change." The parent's question betrays their belief that the goal is to get the child to comply.

Whenever we attempt to get someone to do something, we are exerting our will over that individual. This rarely works, and nearly always creates power struggles. This is especially true when dealing with highly intuitive individuals such as Indigo Children. Like animals, they can sense the fear beneath your desire to control them. They rebel against your attempts to "win," because your fear frightens them. They want you to be peaceful and secure. When you push your children, they become insecure and afraid.

Therefore, whenever you become upset at some aspect of your child's behavior, a first step is to resist the impulse to react immediately. Instead, give yourself a time-out for five or ten minutes. Retreat into the bathroom or some other private location, then close your eyes and breathe deeply. Pray for spiritual intervention from God, your angels, and the ascended masters. An especially powerful method is to envision yourself handing the entire situation over to Spirit. I often visualize angels holding a giant bucket, in which I place anything that is bothering me. Once I feel a peaceful sensation, I know that solutions are forthcoming. This method always results in miracles.

Second, keep your priorities in mind. You *elected* to come to Earth as a lightworker during the millennium shift. You *elected* to parent an Indigo Child. These missions are your top priorities, and everything else rates as less important. When you review your life from the afterlife plane, you will consider the moments in which you modeled love for your children to be your greatest successes. What *won't* matter to you was if your kitchen was perfectly clean or whether your child got good grades. Only love matters.

Third, visualize the type of relationship that you would like to have with your child. I have counseled parents on this method for years, always with great results. One mother was at her wit's end with her daughter. She complained constantly about how "bad" her daughter was behaving. I stopped the mother mid-sentence, and said to her, "You are claiming that your daughter has a lot of faults. Is this what you really want?"

She looked at me as if I were crazy and said, "No, of course not!"

"Well," I replied, "we experience everything that we claim as true. You are claiming that your daughter is misbehaving, and as long as you claim this as your truth, this will be what you experience."

My client, a metaphysically savvy woman, knew instantly what I meant: She had to change her thinking. I helped her visualize her daughter as loving, close, kind, and everything else that my client desired. She visualized with great detail, seeing her daughter and herself going to the movies together, for example. Within days, she reported that her daughter was behaving exactly as she'd visualized. The healing was instantaneous and has lasted over the course of several years now.

Some people may cringe and think, *Isn't this exerting my will over my child?* In truth, I believe this visualization method is a product of our knowledge that we are all one being. There are no separate people, but only an illusion that others are separate from ourselves. Visualization underscores the truth that everyone is an outpicturing of our own thoughts, feelings, and expectations.

After all, don't you behave differently around different people? Aren't you "nicer" around people who obviously like you? Aren't you prone to being in a worse mood when you are around "negative" people? Our children are no different. When we see them as being holy, happy, perfect, and beautiful children of God, they naturally exude those qualities.

Shifting Frequencies with Your Indigo Child

At health food stores and in natural living magazines, you can find herbal and flower-essence "remedies" for ADHD. Probably, these methods work very well. In fact, whatever we *believe* will work *will* always work.

I'm not a big fan of using any external treatment, however. I'm sure that people who espouse drugs and aromatherapy have the purest of intentions, so please don't misunderstand me. My beliefs stem from the philosophy that every condition is an illusion, and that if we diagnose, label, or treat the condition, we make it real. We also make it grow worse.

It's important that we not label or judge our children as being "broken" in any way. Let's even use caution with the term *Indigo Child*, and not let the label have us think of our children as special or different. Every one of God's children is identical, since we are all one. The only difference is this: In this dream of the material world where we appear to be separate, the Indigo Children have a unique mission to fulfill. They are literally people from the future, incarnated into a planet still rooted in the past.

So let's see our Indigo Children from the highest of planes. Let's honor the angel within them, as the channel Kryon always says, just like we honor the angel within ourselves and others. With that in mind, let's co-parent our Indigo Children with God.

I've learned from my conversations with God and the angels that it is vital to take excellent care of our bodies. The reason has nothing to do with vanity or aesthetics; it is purely because well-toned, well-nourished bodies are more receptive to Divine guidance. The spiritual importance of eating a natural diet that is low in meat, or completely without it, is promoted by many of the Eastern orientations, as well as the Pythagorean school of philosophy (the cradle of modern metaphysics and spiritual healing).

The reason for this is that foods carry vibrational frequencies. The higher-frequency foods help the body resonate at a higher rate, so that a person can more easily stay centered in their true-self state. The higher your frequency, the more your natural intuitive abilities will capture the messages of God, your spirit guides, and angels.

Live, fresh foods such as vegetables, fruits, and sprouted grain products have the highest vibrational frequencies. Dead, frozen, dried, or overcooked foods have the lowest vibrational frequencies. Low vibrations are also found in sugar, food coloring, preservatives, and pesticides (which have the energy of death) sprayed on nonorganic foods.

You help yourself and your child attain the highest spiritual frequency, which is necessary for the new energy of the New Age, by eating a largely vegetarian diet, devoid of chemicals. In fact, this is the exact dietary advice given by experts in treating ADHD.

The media outlets—television, magazines, movies, radio, the Internet, and newspapers—also carry vibrational frequencies. Those media based in negativity, fear, or lack have the lowest frequencies. Those that espouse true spiritual love have the highest frequencies. It's important to keep your household as high in frequency as possible. So, curtail all tendencies to have the news playing in your home, and don't keep negative newspapers or magazines lying around. Pray for spiritual intervention and guidance in keeping your child away from negative-themed media. Your prayers will work faster and more effectively than would lectures or reprimands.

Finally, remember the power of forgiveness to effect miracles in all areas of your life, especially in your relationships. As *A Course in Miracles* says, "Do not forget today that there can be no form of suffering that fails to hide an unforgiving thought. Nor can there be a form of pain forgiveness cannot heal."

I find that the issues of parenting an Indigo Child are exacerbated when parents experience marital challenges or messy divorces. Interestingly, following an 18-month study of familial issues connected with ADHD, Patrick J. Kilcarr, Ph.D., and Patricia O. Quinn, M.D., concluded the following:

> The two most critical and influential factors appeared to be a father's attitude toward and belief in his child. Mothers naturally and often unconditionally express their love toward their children, especially children who tend to be more needy and dependent like those who have ADHD. Fathers on the other hand, if they do not understand the way ADHD manifests itself in their children, may express ongoing disappointment that results in an emotional withdrawal.

> Many of the fathers interviewed struggled to determine which behaviors were related to ADHD and which negative behaviors were purposeful on the part of their child. This often led to a heightened sense of frustration in the fathers and an over-focusing on the problematic behaviors. This pattern has the potential for keeping the father and child locked into a cycle of negative interaction. Fathers who reported a deep understanding of the effects of ADHD on their children

generally were able to avoid this type of destructive cycle by focusing on the positive behaviors.

This is not an attempt to blame fathers for any situation. In fact, I've found that if the Indigo Child's mother blames the child's father in any way, the situation grows worse. It's vital for everyone involved with the child to be willing to forgive themselves, the other parent, the child, the teachers, the doctors, and everyone.

When we hold the energy of unforgiveness in our consciousness, we literally are centered in the old energy. We exist, then, in the parallel universe governed by the ego. In that world, problems reign and chaos is triumphant. However, when we are willing to forgive ourselves and the world, we re-center ourselves in the true world of love and Spirit. In this world, everything is harmoniously healed. Fortunately, we don't need to *try* to forgive; we simply need to be *willing* to forgive. This little window of willingness is enough for the light of Spirit to heal us of all false illusions in our thoughts.

Having an Indigo Child is a true gift to the world, and if you approach the situation with Spirit, it is a gift to you and the child. Your child is here to teach you, and vice versa. By having heart-to-heart discussions, you will learn amazing spiritual truths from your child. You'll also develop a greater closeness and sense of trust. And we must always remember that God is the Indigo Child's true mother and father. When we continuously turn to God for co-parenting assistance, raising an Indigo Child becomes a most meaningful and enjoyable part of our Divine life purpose.[5]

Spiritual Evolution

We are learning from metaphysicians and their sources that these new children entering the planet are far more spiritually aware. This doesn't mean that all Indigos are going to grow into ministers and spiritual giants. It does mean that they arrive with a different awareness than we did.

Why would this be, if it's true at all? Again, according to most spiritual sources, not only were the kids expected, but they are proof of an evolution in human consciousness, beyond the "old energy" of previous generations. They are peacemakers, wise old souls, and a supreme hope for better things on this planet. They are interested in making things peaceful at home between parents. They *care,* far beyond the expected norms for children, and are spouting wisdom that makes us speechless. Their humanitarian instincts come "built in," and show themselves from the beginning. They know they belong. They are a new evolutionary step in humanity.

We don't know about you, but we want to nurture these peacemakers! We want to give them every consideration to be exactly what they came to be—the hope of a far better planet consciousness than we ever thought possible.

Many spiritual and religious historians are taking note of this planetary phenomenon and believe that it actually triggers a change in overall prophecy. It speaks of a far greater chance for humanity—far beyond the millennium change. It voids some of the worst-case predicted endings that old scriptures tell us about, and reinforces other spiritual information that says humans can make a difference in their own destiny—change the future and move past fear and hate. It gives us hope that all the doom-and-gloom predictions about the year 2000 are now just so much drivel in the age of the Indigo.

We can't think of a better way to meld into the next chapter than to present a story from **Laurie Joy Pinkham.** Laurie comes to you in these pages as a mom, but she also holds a degree in early childhood education from the University of New Hampshire, as well as her Doctorate of Divinity.

Laurie shares the story of her Indigo Children's experiences and struggles. Although she speaks of spiritual things, you are going to notice still another reference to ADD and ADHD. Why is this medical diagnosis springing up all over this book? What does it have to do with Indigo Children?

Here is Laurie's story. Keep it in mind as you read in the next chapter about Ritalin, the ADD diagnosis, and alternate health suggestions for all the misdiagnosed Indigos.

My Dear Indigos!
Rev. Dr. Laurie Joy Pinkham

I have raised two Indigo Children, and my three granddaughters are also Indigos. My sons were born in the '70s, and my granddaughters in this decade. Raising them has been no easy task over the years. I always knew that there was something very different with both sons—each one an individual, but each one very different from their peers.

Mark, my older son, has always been sensitive and very detached from most people. As an infant he would lay, literally for hours, in his crib and "talk" to the mobile

and stuffed animals. He did not like to be held or cud-
dled, but preferred the comfort of the "unseen" guides
and the confines of his crib.

Mark's verbal skills were clear at a very early age. He
could talk in sentences by the time he was 18 months old.
By the time he was two, he was a whiz at building with
Legos® and Lincoln Logs® and he loved music, particularly Mozart, Chopin, Beethoven, and all the Baroque music.

Scott, my younger son, was very attached and very
unhappy to be here. From the moment he took his first
breath, he cried and cried. It seemed as though this lasted for three years. For the first nine months of his life he
slept very little. As a matter of fact, he was carried in a
Snuggli® for most of this time. The comfort of my heartbeat and the warmth and closeness of my body seemed to
be the only thing that nurtured and comforted him,
allowing a feeling of safety so that he could sleep for brief
periods of time.

The most difficult attribute of raising these children
was that I had no resources to help me. I would look at
other parents and wonder what was the matter with my
children. Why did they act this way? We had no close
friends since our children were not "the norm," and thus
folks did not invite us to their homes. We all felt isolated.

I have always loved children and have always known
that I would have at least two. In an attempt to understand my children better, I earned a degree in early childhood education, and in the 1980s I operated a child-care
program. During this time, I observed children of varied
backgrounds. These children would tell some of the
wildest stories about their angels, guides, and imaginary
friends. I loved listening to them, and it was a great comfort to know that someday these children would be considered the norm, and that these stories were the reality
that we would come to understand.

Both of my children have been unusual in the sense
of their experiences. Scott used to wake me up at night to
go outside and look at the spaceships he was seeing. I

would get up, go outside, and just listen to him describe what he was seeing. Of course, I saw nothing! I knew this was important to him, and it was not a good idea for him to be alone outside in the middle of the night at age seven. During this time, which lasted until he was 14, we would talk about all the metaphysical things that he knew.

His brother Mark would call me into his room at night and ask if I could see the spaceman standing there, or the flying saucers. Of course, again, I could not see them, but I really wanted to. I would wait, hoping that I too would be able to see them. I look back now and wonder if all along it was my children who awakened me.

In 1984, after tremendous difficulty in school, Scott was diagnosed with ADHD (back then it was ADDH). I did not know anything about this, but immersed myself in learning. As I read, I realized that Mark too was ADD, but without the hyperactivity factor. Thus began a whole new approach to parenting—understanding and working to make their lives and ours as peaceful as possible. Not an easy task! There were no resources.

Our children played all the usual sports, which brought us all together. It also gave them a sense of belonging. For most of their younger lives, they had been social outcasts; fighting and reactive behavior had been their only ways to cope. They could not understand why these things happened to them, and both were saddened at the lack of understanding with their peers.

We tried various forms of medications, which each worked for extended periods. Ritalin and Dexadrine were the top choices in the medical field at that time. There were no homeopathic doctors in our area, and alternative medicine was not widely accepted or accessible in 1983.

We went to several specialists looking for answers to help both children, most times hitting brick walls, and the advice given was to use very restricted and controlled behavior regimes that just never felt right and created much hatred within the family structure when we tried them. They also created even more behavioral problems.

I found that accepting their difference was the first step in trying to help them. After all, these children led the way for many more ADD and ADHD children that followed them. I helped to form a local support group for parents whose children were having the same experiences, which led to the founding of the New Hampshire chapter of Children with Attention Deficit Disorder (CH.A.D.D.).[65] The beauty of this was the shared experiences of the parents. We could talk about the frustrations that we all were collectively experiencing, and problem-solve by trial and error.

As my children grew into adolescence, it became more difficult to help them. The usual adolescent behaviors, when coupled with their medical diagnosis and learning disabilities, began to wear us all down. The school system was only structured to be punitive, not supportive, in its approach. They did not understand these way-showers, but only tried to control behavior.

When Mark was 15, he talked to us about going to live with a friend, and we decided to give it a try. Things were not working well at home, so we hoped that the separation might help, but instead the situation worsened.

Mark got into difficulties that led to his placement in a children's group home. This compounded the behavior problems. He was placed there because of his impulsive behavior and wanting to be like everyone else. He could never see the consequences of his intended actions. He literally just did not get it. After the fact, his face would always be so blank, as if he couldn't believe he hadn't realized that what he was doing would get him into trouble. This first series of incidents involved shoplifting *The Book of Runes,* and then a few weeks later, on a dare, he stole a friend's father's car.

When he was released from the group home, he was in and out of difficult situations for a few years. Always these involved the inability to see the consequences of his intended actions. He became saddened and hardened. As a parent, I was lost regarding how to support him, without enabling the behaviors. I knew that his essence was wonderful, but dealing with the behavioral problems of a hormonally imbalanced ADD male child was beyond my experience.

Scott, my younger son, was a tough one, too. He excelled in sports, particularly hockey, as well as music, art, and writing imaginary stories; however, the rest of school presented many difficulties for him. He never saw gray areas. His social behaviors were always competitive. He always wanted to win, whether at board games or in discussions.

On the winter solstice in 1991, I visited Mark at the apartment he shared with friends, and brought over a "care" package. (The last time I visited, they only had hot dogs, bologna, and beer in the refrigerator.) As I entered the front door, I noticed with amazement a statue of Christ at the top of the stairs. I recognized it from the church down the road.

I told the boys, since they were both involved in the incident, that they had 48 hours to return the Christ to the church, or I would call the police and tell them where the statue was. Each day I called the rectory, and each day I received the same answer: "No, the statue has not been returned."

On the third day, I called the local police and reported the location of the statue. They went to Mark's apartment, retrieved the statue, and arrested him. Mark was no longer a minor, so he landed in county jail for one year.

It is interesting as I look back on this time. Mark was released on bail pending a hearing. He "missed" his hearing and was arrested on January 11, 1992—this was the 11:11, a metaphysically significant date on which a spiritual gateway to enlightenment was activated.

Five months later, Scott's guilt forced him to confess to actually being the one who stole the statue; he had brought it to Mark's apartment. He went to the courthouse and confessed to a judge that he was the one who had done it, and he was placed in a children's home for 90 days.

My marriage was also ending at this time. As parents, my husband and I were at a loss as to how to help these children. It was, as I look back, a real opening in my own life. All of this—reporting my son, pulling away from my marriage, the police arriving at the 11:11 celebration, and my spiritual awakening—had flowed from the point when I became a Reiki Master in 1988. I know now that my son Mark and I had a contract. Now we talk about this openly and with laughter. We healed a very difficult time in our lives, and we know that we could have done it differently, but this was what we chose.

In 1997, Mark was again in the county jail for traffic violations, speeding tickets, leaving the scene of an accident, and unpaid fines. During this time, I was guided to not go and visit him. I was "told" to wait and give him time to understand the consequences of this behavior, that this was a learning time for him and his next awakening.

Six months before his release, I was guided to start sending him books. I sent him all the Kryon books by Lee Carroll, as well as the *Conversations with God* books. He read all of this, admittedly as a captive audience, but he started sharing them with other inmates—they would read the material and discuss it! I felt as if our spirits had come full circle: from the early awakening of my being open to the spacemen and guides and angels, through his awakenings in a county jail, to his awakening others who listened. A way-shower!

Now out of jail, Mark is a Reiki facilitator, working and raising his two daughters, Kathryn and Emma, and he has a new approach to life. He struggles with the differences in himself, but is also opening to a new understanding of who he is. I am convinced that this early Indigo Child is here to help others, and to be a father to two young women who are here to make a difference.

Scott is working in the medical field and has one child, Kayley, whom I call "Kibit." When Kibit was born, I *knew* it, although I was several states away, and I was racing back to be there in time. I was not surprised, when I picked up my messages, that Scott was calling from the hospital. I went there and witnessed the birth of Kayley Isabel.

This child "spoke" to me moments after she was born. She was in great distress, and they were going to airlift her to a major medical center. I held her and told her that if she needed to go back to the spirit world, it was okay. It was then that she told me that she was here to see me and that it would be four months before we saw each other again. This was all communicated through looking into each other's eyes.

Scott and I got into a disagreement, and it was indeed four months before I was to hold Kibit again. Scott started to tell me stories about her—how he was always feeling that she could see everything about him. I remember him saying that he thought she could read his thoughts and that she would just stare at him all the time. As she grew older, her verbal skills and independence were very obvious. At 14 months, she talked in full sentences. She knew where she came from and would tell me. She would sit in her crib and just stare and "talk" without opening her mouth.

Scott himself has always been "lucky." He has just always innately known when he was going to win or lose, and he has almost always been right on. He talks with me a lot about Kayley, because he knows that she too is different.

Until more folks started talking about Indigo Children, none of us had a reference for who these unusual, sometimes misunderstood, often very gifted children were. I feel such a sense of wonder to see the next generation of these wonderful beings. They know what they want and who they are, and they are not at all shy about asking or telling you this. They talk of being here before and knowing who you were before. Kayley speaks of this to me now. She tells me about her angels and guides and what they are telling her. Scott listens to his daughter and now understands why he struggled growing up.

Emma, Mark's daughter, is still young, but she shows signs of being Indigo. She talks and has incredibly fine motor skills. Her body is long and flexible. Her eyes always sparkle, and she points to the invisible things that I still can't see, but I know that she is telling me who she is seeing around me and that these beings are my guides and angels. She smiles at them, talks to them . . . then looks me in the eyes and silently tells me who I am.

Mark's other daughter, Kathryn Elizabeth, talks of the pet angel that she has. She smiles and holds out her hand, and off they walk to the sandbox to dig tunnels and make mud pies and talk about the days ahead.

It has helped me to know that my children are indeed gifts. We have had contracts together throughout time, and it is indeed a blessing to know that it continues with my granddaughters. I love my sons so very much, and I still tell them how incredibly special they are. I tell them that I am grateful that we had the rough times and that the journey has made us all closer. I know that my children have shown the way for many. They have awakened my soul on its journey, and they have created my granddaughters—who know, indeed, exactly who they are!

More Indigo Stories

When my daughter Marlyn was barely three years old, we were saying the prayer together out loud that begins, "Now I lay me down to sleep. . . ." At the conclusion, Marlyn asked me what prayer I usually said, and asked that I repeat it out loud. I began the Lord's prayer, and she joined in immediately. I know she had not been exposed to this before, at least not in her current body, so I asked her how she knew the prayer so well. She told me she used to say it "all the time." I congratulated her on remembering so well.

We had quite a discourse on how strong some of these memories could be and how important it was to respect them. This type of conversation was not unusual, and I considered it quite the norm, having had no sisters or brothers and few experiences with such young children. Only when friends would draw my attention to the extremely adult manner of our conversations was I even aware that this was not the norm.

On one occasion, she was in her car seat in back while a friend rode in the front with me. My friend and I were discussing some of the more esoteric constructs of a temple we attended, how some seemed to be so egocentric to the figurehead of the organization, and yet the underlying truth was present, without doubt. Marlyn piped up that we should make an effort to understand each other, as well as "the truth" (obviously referring to the figurehead whom we were discussing). My friend was aghast; however, I recognized as a matter of course that since Marlyn is such an old soul, it is quite natural for her to identify this need.

— Terry Smith, mother of Marlyn, now age 12

My 15-year-old daughter, Stef, and I live in a rural, Dutch-traditional religious community. I know there is a place for our words, and I pray we will be led to it.

We were talking about what the kids in school thought of heaven, and she said, "Heaven is another word to describe the place after—but it is still limiting."

Discussing heaven, she said, "God has not stopped creating—the universe is changing. He is building people and things to learn to love him."

Discussing predestination, she said, "God doesn't know what you're going to do. He built you with love and His knowledge. You have to do what you think is right. You have destiny, but do you want it? If you hit somebody, God does not plan that for you; it's your choice. God had a thought—He created humankind, and humankind tried to get that thought. I am now the thought and I am now human. I am both a part of God and the creation. I am the Creator and the Creation."

— Laurie Werner, mother of Stef, age 15

Our Indigo Child

*I look in your eyes, and I'm held by your stare.
So much knowledge—so alert and aware.*

*I feel that I know you, I've met you before.
Where have you come from? I want to know more.*

*Do you remember a faraway place,
with a different name and a different face?*

*Don't be upset if we don't understand
the message you bring with you back to this land.*

*We know who you are; we know why you are here.
To answer our questions your purpose is clear.*

*I know that you feel that you don't belong here.
Don't be frustrated—we'll always be near.*

*Our family is close in both spirit and mind.
We understand you, and we know of your kind.*

*You offer us love, and you bind us together.
Your touch on our hearts is as light as a feather.*

*Why have you chosen to be our little girl?
What is the message you bring to our world?*

*Your spirit is gentle, so peaceful and mild.
Your spirit is special, our Indigo Child.*

— by Mark Denny, written for his daughter, Savannah, age two

c h a p t e r   f o u r

Health Issues

This chapter is *not* specifically about ADD (Attention Deficit Disorder) or ADHD (Attention Deficit Hyperactive Disorder). There is a great amount of truly outstanding information available today on that subject, and we are not going to pretend to be authorities on all that it involves. However, because the drug Ritalin is being used so widely to treat children who may simply be Indigo, we want you to be aware of the very latest information available regarding this drug.

If you turned to this chapter expecting to find alternative, nondrug treatments for those who are truly ADD or ADHD, we might have that, also. But this chapter is dedicated to those who have been misdiagnosed with ADD or ADHD, when all they really are is Indigo Children! In many cases, what works for ADD also works for the Indigo experience, especially in nutrition and alternate behavior systems.

Let's repeat some information that has been woven throughout this book:

1. Not all Indigo Children are ADD or ADHD!

2. Not all ADD or ADHD children are Indigo!

Before we present our piece of the puzzle, we wish to honor those who are the leaders in ADD and ADHD research and are helping the planet with their writings. There are many, but below are just a few selections from the bestseller lists of retail booksellers—mainstream ADD books that are helping literally millions of parents. Perhaps after this book is published, we will have a listing of more books that apply specifically to Indigos. If so, you may find them on our Internet site at: **www.Indigochild.com.**

Some Recommended ADD and ADHD Books

1. *Driven to Distraction,* by Edward Hallowell, M.D. This book is considered by many to be the best book in the medical approach to ADD.[58]

2. *Helping Your Hyperactive ADD Child,* by John F. Taylor. Another wonderful work, considered to be the most comprehensive writing on the subject of ADD and ADHD children.[59]

3. *Raising Your Spirited Child,* by Mary Sheedy Kurcinka. This book covers how to deal with certain characteristics from a parenting perspective.[60]

4. *The A.D.D. Book,* by William Sears, M.D., and Lynda Thompson, Ph.D. This book, written by a pediatrician and a child psychologist, outlines a drug-free approach to treating children with ADD.[61]

5. *Running on Ritalin,* by Lawrence Diller. You really should read this if you are currently using Ritalin with your children.[62]

6. *No More Ritalin: Treating ADHD Without Drugs,* by Mary Ann Block. Block's book actually represents what this chapter is about.[63]

7. *Ritalin: Its Use and Abuse,* by Eileen Beal.[64] (Not actually published at the writing of this book, but reviewed.)

There are also organizations operating specifically to help *you* with your ADD child. The most visible at the writing of this book is **CH.A.D.D.**[65] (Children with Attention Deficit Disorder). This organization invites your call and has information collected and organized from all over the nation. Consider them a hub of consolidated up-to-date information providers. Their website is a good resource to check out.

Another wonderful organization is **Network of Hope.**[66] This Florida-based group is a nonprofit corporation founded by a group of concerned citizens. From their website: "We all agree that 'our children are our greatest resource.' We are a *heart*-connected group of people in North America who choose to *embrace* others and to share this *hope* with all families." Their website is also a good resource for nutritional information.

Are You Curing or Numbing?

So far in this book, you have heard parents talk about being at their wit's end, having children that seem to be ADD, but aren't quite. Some have had their children diagnosed as ADD and have gone through the routine with the appropriate drugs. As we mentioned before, this has seemed to help—but did it help the parents or the children? Sure, some children may have calmed down and may have conformed, but was it because their "evolved consciousness" was numbed out?

This chapter is for those of you who are wondering if your child is truly ADD, or perhaps one of the new Indigos. We are going to present some information from **Dr. Doreen Virtue** on the diagnosis of ADD and the Indigos, then some alternative treatments to ADD that we've found in our travels, which are also useful for Indigos who are having trouble with the world around them.

Some of the alternatives might seem odd—but we would not include them here unless we knew they were *working!*

Is Compliance Healthy?
Doreen Virtue, Ph.D.

Indigo Children are often diagnosed as ADHD because they refuse to comply. When we watch a Clint Eastwood movie, we applaud his rebel nature. Yet when this same spirit is evident in children, we give them drugs.

Therapist Russell Barkley, author of *Hyperactive Children: A Handbook for Diagnosis and Treatment*,[67] writes: "Although inattention, overactivity, and poor impulse control are the most common symptoms cited by others as primary in hyperactive children, my own work with these children suggests that *noncompliance is also a primary problem.*"

I have worked in the psychiatric field for many years. I remember, as a counselor intern, working for a prominent psychiatrist. Every day, his waiting room was filled with dozens of people who patiently sat while the doctor consistently ran one hour late for his appointments. He would see each patient for a maximum of ten minutes, typing notes across a big desk while the patient talked. At the end of each session, he would write a prescription.

At first, I must admit that I judged this doctor for giving drug treatment instead of using verbal therapy. Then I realized that he was simply doing what doctors do. If you give a person a hammer, he or she will pound on things. If you consult a medical doctor, he or she will invariably prescribe drugs as the answer to whatever ails you. It reminds me of that old axiom "Never try to teach a pig to sing. You'll waste your time and annoy the pig." In other words, people are what they are. So it's no wonder that when educators, fed up with noncompliance, refer children to child psychiatrists and family physicians, Ritalin is given.

However, in all fairness, there are some psychiatrists who publicly condemn the use of Ritalin. "Ritalin does not correct biochemical imbalances—it causes them," reveals Peter R. Breggin, M.D., director of the International Center for the Study of Psychiatry and Psychology and associate faculty member at The Johns Hopkins University Department of Counseling.[68] He states:

> ADHD is a controversial diagnosis with little or no scientific or medical basis. A parent, teacher, or doctor can feel in good company when utterly dismissing the diagnosis and refusing to apply it to children.
> There is no proof of any physical abnormalities in the brains or bodies of children who are routinely labeled ADHD. They do not have known biochemical imbalances or "crossed wires."

Dr. Breggin adds that there is some evidence that Ritalin can cause permanent damage to the child's brain and its function. Ritalin decreases blood flow to the brain, and routinely causes other gross malfunctions in the developing brain of a child. He continues:

> Children don't have disorders; they live in a disordered world. . . . When adults provide them a better environment, they tend to quickly improve their outlook and behavior. But, children and teenagers can eventually become so upset, confused, and self-destructive that they internalize the pain or become compulsively rebellious. They should never be given the idea that they are

diseased or defective, as the primary cause of their con-
flicts is with their schools and families.

Children can benefit from guidance in learning to be
responsible for their own conduct; but they do not gain
from being blamed for the trauma and stress that they are
exposed to in the environment around them. They need
empowerment, not humiliating diagnoses and mind-
disabling drugs. Most of all, they thrive when adults show
concern and attention to their basic needs as children.

Different Approaches for Indigo Children

The primary task for all of us is to cocoon ourselves and
our children from the tail end of the old energy that we now
reside within. Instead of drugging our children, or forcing
them to comply with old energy standards, there are alternative ways to create harmony within Indigo Children's
households.

For example, Mary Ann Block, D.O., author of the book,
No More Ritalin: Treating ADHD Without Drugs,[63] treats
ADHD-diagnosed children by understanding their unique
ways of thinking. She has observed that these children are
primarily right-brained. That is, they are oriented toward
being visual, creative, artistic, physical, and spatial. Our
educational system, which demands a librarian-like left-
brain approach, doesn't comply well with the natural thinking styles of right-brain dominant children.

According to Dr. Block, "The children also tend to be
tactile learners." This means that they learn best with their
hands. In the early years of school, because these children
are often very smart, they are able to compensate. But by
the fourth or fifth grade, the teacher stands in front of the
class, lecturing and writing assignments on the black
board. The children are expected to take notes and write
assignments down correctly. But these children have difficulty learning in this classroom setting. She writes:

Although they see and hear the information, the brain doesn't process the information through the auditory and visual senses as well. These children are still going to try to learn, but because they are tactile learners, they may pick up their pencil and flip it, put their hands in their pockets, or put their hands on the person in front of them. Then they get in trouble, when all they were trying to do was learn the best way they know how, through touch. So even though they are very bright, they very often get labeled as learning disabled or troublemakers.

When Dr. Block says that these children are tactile and feeling-oriented, she is referring to their natural clairsentient abilities. This means that the Indigo Children receive and send information through their emotional and physical feelings. Clairsentience is a form of psychic communication that is often called *intuition or telepathy.* I believe that everyone is naturally telepathic and that, in the new world, we will all regain this ability. Let's not punish the Indigo Children for retaining a skill that we would all benefit from having! Dr. Block continues:

Because tactile learners sometimes have trouble learning through their auditory and visual senses, they often need tactile stimulation to help them learn through their other senses. This means they may need something to touch while they are looking and listening. We provide a small, soft, squeezable ball for children to use. Your child should be allowed to handle the ball or another object with one hand while listening, reading or writing, whether in school or at home. Invoking the tactile senses while trying to learn may enhance their auditory and visual learning. This may also reduce unacceptable, active behavior in the classroom.

Tactile learners may not hear a parent when they call them or talk to them. Call their name first to try to get the child's attention before giving them a verbal directive. If you are close to your child, gently touch him/her on the shoulder or arm in order to help "ground" the information, and then give them the directive verbally.

What to Do?

Okay. So a child may be either ADD or Indigo or both. Either way, we know that you as a parent have to deal with imbalance in your house, day in and day out. What can you do about it? Sitting and wondering doesn't help you or your kid! Perhaps you have already taken action. Perhaps, before you ever started treating your child, you studied ADD, had meetings with other parents, and went to doctors. We honor you for that, and would expect this kind of caring. Now we are telling you that there is still something more! But our intention is to give you hope—not to add to your confusion.

We wish to establish something right now: None of these contributors or authors are trying to make any parent feel guilty for placing their child on a drug. We aren't here to point a finger and make anyone "wrong." We merely wish to present to you an argument about what Ritalin is, and also make you aware of alternate treatment. We also wish you to consider that perhaps your child isn't ADD or ADHD after all. If any of the information so far "fits" your child, then we feel you might wish to learn about what some others are doing.

Healers, educators, and child-industry workers have filled this chapter with reports about solutions to problems that seem to have ADD and ADHD symptoms (which, as established, also fit many Indigos). These methods are not all accepted, but, as we know, revolutionary cures are usually snubbed at first! Recent history is filled with examples of this. We are reminded of the revelation about the cure for ulcers—the discovery that they are caused by bacteria. The medical industry hooted and hollered until the last minute about that one. It was only after the doctor who discovered it almost killed himself proving it on his own body that the drug companies finally "came on board." This book may be presenting something similar; only time will tell.

We wish to present some reports and facts about Ritalin. Some of this is new information, some old, but all of it is very important for you to know. *Time* magazine recently devoted their main section to Ritalin, saying:

> The pace at which Ritalin use has been growing has alarmed critics for a while now. Some doctors find themselves battling anxious parents who, worried that their child will daydream his future away, demand the drug, and if refused, go off to find a more cooperative physician. Some parents feel pressured to medicate their child just so that his behavior will conform a bit more to other children's, even if they are quite content with their child's conduct—quirks, tantrums and all. . . .
>
> Production of Ritalin has increased more than sevenfold in the past eight years, and 90% of it is consumed in the U.S. Such figures invite the charge that school districts, insurance companies and overstressed families are turning to medication as a quick fix for complicated problems that might be better addressed by smaller classes, psychotherapy or family counseling, or basic changes in the hectic environment that so many American children face every day. . . .
>
> Even doctors who have seen Ritalin's positive, sometimes miraculous effects warn that the drug is no substitute for better schools, creative teaching and parents' spending more time with their kids. Unless a child acquires coping skills, the benefits of medication are gone as soon as it wears off. . . .
>
> The trend over the past few years has been clear: the percentage of children with an ADHD (or ADD) diagnosis

walking out of a doctor's office with a prescription jumped from 55% in 1989 to 75% in 1996.[1]

In mainstream science and medicine, we are beginning to see "Ritalin alarm," and some common sense and alternate approaches to children diagnosed as ADD or ADHD. Basic technical questions about this commonly used drug are beginning to be asked: What is the *real* story on how Ritalin works? How would you like to know what the doctors know? Are there side effects? What do the experts say?

Here is what J. Zink, Ph.D., a California family therapist and the author of several books on raising children, had to say, as quoted in the same issue of *Time*: "Let's not deny Ritalin works. But why does it work, and what are the consequences of overprescribing? The reality is we don't know."[1]

The following, written in 1984, echoes the same sentiment. It's from *How to Raise a Healthy Child . . . in Spite of Your Doctor,* by Robert Mendelsohn, M.D.[69]

> No one has ever been able to demonstrate that drugs such as Cylert and Ritalin improve the academic performance of the children who take them. The major effect of Ritalin and similar drugs is on the short-term manageability of hyperkinetic behavior. The pupil is drugged to make life easier for his teacher, not to make it better and more productive for the child. If your child is the victim, the potential risks of these drugs is a high price to pay to make his teacher more comfortable.

With this in mind, consider the following quote from a 1998 meeting of the National Institutes of Health, taken from the same issue of *Time*. Very little has changed regarding Ritalin in 15 years!

Ritalin clearly works in the short term to reduce the symptoms of ADHD. But more and more kids have been taking the drug for years, and no studies have run long enough to see if it has a lasting effect on academic performance or social behavior.

Ritalin can interfere with a child's growth rate, although the latest research suggests that it only delays—rather than stunts—a youngster's development. While there has been an increase in the number of stimulant prescriptions for children under five, there is no evidence that these drugs are safe or effective used on young children.[1]

Side Effects of Ritalin

What we next discuss may be entirely new to you—only doctors normally see it. It may give you chills—we hope so. As quoted by Robert Mendelsohn, M.D., in his book *How to Raise a Healthy Child . . . in Spite of Your Doctor,*[69] the following entry is taken word for word from *The Physician's Desk Reference.* The entry is supplied by the manufacturer of Ritalin, Ciba-Geigy, as required by law.

As you read the following report, note that the company acknowledges that it *does not know how Ritalin works,* or how its effects relate to the condition of the central nervous system. It admits that its long-term safety is unknown. As you read, note that the parenthetical comments are supplied by Dr. Mendelsohn.

> Nervousness and insomnia are the most common adverse reactions but are usually controlled by reducing dosage and omitting the drug in the afternoon and the evening. Other reactions include hypersensitivity (including skin rash), urticaria (swollen, itching patches of skin), fever, arthralgia, exfoliative dermatitis (scaly patches of skin), erythema multiforme (an acute inflammatory skin disease), with histopathological find-

ings of necrotizing vasculitis (destruction of the blood vessels), and thrombocytopenic purpura (a serious blood clotting disorder), anorexia; nausea; dizziness; palpitations; headache; dyskinesia (impairment of voluntary muscle movement), drowsiness; blood pressure and pulse changes, both up and down; tachycardia (rapid heartbeat), angina (spasmodic attacks of intense heart pain); cardiac arrhythmia (irregular heartbeat); abdominal pain, weight loss during prolonged therapy.

There have been rare reports of Tourette's syndrome. Toxic psychosis has been reported in patients taking this drug; leukopenia (reduction in white blood cells) and/or anemia; a few instances of scalp hair loss. In children, loss of appetite, abdominal pain, weight loss during prolonged therapy, insomnia, and tachycardia may occur more frequently; however, any of the other adverse reactions listed above may also occur.

What now follows is about new substances, "far out" forms of therapy, and much useful information on nutrition. We begin with a report from **Keith Smith,**[70] an iridologist and herbalist in California who has been having phenomenal success using very unorthodox methods, some of which hardly anyone is aware of. Some of his report is technical for those who want that, but we have also asked for case histories, which we believe everyone can understand.

We asked Keith to present his methods and also address the Indigo and ADD conundrum specifically. Again, we would not present any information without first seeing it work! Today's "far out" theories are often tomorrow's science.

Chronic Reversed Polarity in Today's Special Children
Keith R. Smith

For all children, our aim should be to cure rather than to treat. While reviewing information on ADD, ADHD, and learning disabilities (LD), I was shocked to find a report on the efforts of the National Institute of Child Health and Human Development (NICHD). This organization reports in their summary that "support for projects related to learning and language disabilities has increased from 1.75 million in 1975 to over 15 million in 1993." A cumulative total of approximately 80 million dollars in research alone.[71]

Under the title "Future Research Directions in LD," and the subtitle "Treatment/Intervention," is this statement:

> Review of the literature related to reading disabilities and other learning disabilities indicates that no single treatment/intervention approach or method is likely to yield clinically significant, long-term, therapeutic gains with children diagnosed with LD. Unfortunately, to date, there exists scant scientific support for the use of particular interventions or combinations of interventions with different types of learning disabilities.[72]

According to my calculations, this one organization has funded $155 million in research without remedy. Another document from the Internet [mediconsult.com][73] estimates that there are three to five million ADHD children. By adding in those with learning disabilities, the figure rises to 10 million or more children. In this document, the National Institute of Mental Health (NIMH)—the federal agency that supports nationwide research on the brain, mental illness, and mental health—states:

> ADHD has become a national priority. During the 1990s—which the President and Congress have declared the "Decade of the Brain"—it is possible that scientists will pinpoint the biological basis of ADHD and learn how to prevent or treat it even more effectively.

If one organization spends $155 million and there are other government agencies spending millions, I wonder just how much money and research time has been spent with no cure yet in sight.

I am an herbalist and a holistic health practitioner. The reason I was so shocked by all the above information is that in my professions, ADD or ADHD is generally considered one of the easier conditions to improve or alleviate. (We are not medical doctors; therefore, we do not *cure*, but we are allowed to improve wellness and alleviate symptoms within the scope of our practice.) In this report, I have included three case studies; however, it would not be difficult to produce 300 to 3,000 similar case studies. I cannot remember a case of ADD or ADHD that did not produce positive results such as those included, unless the remedies recommended were not taken by the client.

Chronic Reversed Polarity

I discovered chronic reversed polarity (CRP) as a remedy for chronic fatigue syndrome years ago by "accident." Since then, I have come to realize that many of the symptoms of ADHD in children were identical to the symptoms of CRP as it occurs in adults.

When I began testing ADHD children, my suspicions were confirmed. Nearly all ADHD children that have come to my office have chronic reversed polarity. Once I added the standard herbal remedy for this condition to my prior nutritional plan, wonderful things began to happen for the children. They began to respond to the process and improve. Most of them became "well."

Every system and process in the physical body is electrical. Our mental processes, the immune system, and the heart are all part of a vast system that runs electrically. The human body is a self-contained, self-generating electrical system. Whenever electricity is in operation, magnetic fields are created. Magnetic fields have *polarity*: That is, they have a north and south pole. If you put a magnet under stress, it will reverse its polarity; in essence, the north and south poles change positions.

Since the human body is electrical and has a subtle magnetic field, certain conditions such as stress will reverse its north and south poles, its polarity, much like a magnet. This can be temporary, and is treated as such by the vast majority of the holistic/alternative medicine professionals. In my practice, however, I have found that polarity reversal is often long-lasting and can be difficult to heal without a full understanding of the varied presentations.

I was led to discover that polarity reversal often becomes chronic and appears to be a major factor in the cause of chronic fatigue syndrome, depression, anxiety, fibromyalgia, auto immune diseases, cancer, ADHD, and many other conditions that do not seem to "heal" with standard treatments. The varied disease processes and symptoms create confusion in how to treat this problem, which generally goes unnoticed until symptoms become pronounced.

The Body's Electrical System

The condition of reversed polarity weakens the "electrical power" of the body. Prolonged stress is a major cause of this. As the body's electrical charge weakens, symptoms occur as warning signals. If the body's charge falls below 42 hertz, the immune system cannot resist disease. In the early stages of CRP, the body's warning signals may include a backache, pulled muscle, or headache; if we don't listen to these symptoms and slow down to "recharge" our electrical power, the symptoms may worsen to, for example, extreme fatigue, depression, anxiety, migraine headaches, fibromyalgia, numbness, or chronic pain in a weak area.

With reversed polarity, the normal self-preservation system becomes inactive. The usual electrical signals to the immune system seem to destroy instead of protect.

Author's note to healers: In diseases such as ITP (interstitial thrombocytopenic purpura), the Merck manual's description reads: A disease where the spleen mysteriously starts to destroy red blood cells. To slow this often incurable condition, the spleen is removed. A statement in this description states, "It appears that the red blood cells take on an opposite electrical charge. . . ."

Could it be that reversing our electrical charge in the body's weak areas is actually a last-attempt to correct destructive stress conditions that force us into more restful states, such as wheelchairs, homes, or hospital beds?

Some of the major symptoms of CRP exactly parallel ADHD symptoms; for example, poor short-term memory and lack of concentration. I generally get a positive response to the description of feeling "fog-brained." Another helpful diagnostic is to ask the patient to imagine that their brain is a light bulb, and to name the place that uses the most energy and burns the brightest. I then ask them if they have ever experienced a "brownout," or could imagine how they would feel if their lights went dim. The normal adult reply is, "That's exactly how I feel!"

Imagine the handicap a school-age child would have with a "dim brain," considering that schoolwork primarily requires concentration and a good short-term memory.

Nine Symptoms Required for Diagnosis

According to the diagnostic guidelines of the American Psychiatric Association, a diagnosis of ADD or ADHD requires nine symptoms of inattention or nine symptoms of hyperactivity/impulsivity, which have developed before age seven, have persisted for at least six months, and are severe enough to interfere with normal social or school activities. The specific symptoms are:

Inattention

1. Pays little attention to details and makes careless mistakes.
2. Has difficulty paying attention.
3. Does not listen when spoken to.
4. Fails to follow through or finish tasks.
5. Has difficulty getting organized.
6. Avoids tasks requiring sustained mental effort or concentration.
7. Often loses things needed for school or other daily tasks.
8. Is easily distracted.
9. Is often forgetful in daily activities.

Hyperactivity/Impulsivity

1. Often fidgets or squirms.
2. Often leaves seat when staying put is expected.
3. Runs about or climbs on things in inappropriate settings.
4. Has difficulty engaging in quiet play or other activities.
5. Is constantly on the go or appears to be driven by a motor.
6. Talks excessively.
7. Blurts out answer prematurely.
8. Has difficulty awaiting turn.
9. Often interrupts or intrudes on others.

Iris Analysis: Flower and Jewel Types

The Rayid technique of analyzing the eye's iris is too detailed to be fully described here, but briefly, the iris type known as a *Flower*, or emotional type, would correlate more commonly with inattention in a child, and depression in an adult. The iris type known as *Jewel* would correlate more commonly with hyperactivity or impulsivity in a child, and anxiety in an adult.

Utilizing reversed polarity, nutritional analysis, Rayid, and other techniques by complementary alternative practitioners, our unique and special children can receive an accurate analysis. Consideration on a case-by-case basis, utilizing individual symptoms, often produces highly successful results, as shown in the following case studies.

First Case Study

Patient: Female child, age four years, with typical ADD/ADHD symptoms.

History: This child was born seven weeks premature, and spent five days isolated in a neonatal intensive care unit. Her mother said that she had always been "unhealthy and upset," seldom sleeping longer than three hours at a time. This child was very emotional, and during our initial visit appeared to have the classic symptoms of ADHD. Her mother also reported that she had frequent episodes of vomiting and night sweats.

Medical treatment: After undergoing testing and being given a diagnosis of hyperactivity and ADD, Ritalin was suggested if the symptoms continued when the child started school. Her parents chose to seek alternatives to drug therapy.

Complementary alternative: This special child appeared, prebirth, to her parents in a dream, during which she had given them her beautiful and unusual name. She was a *Stream/Flower* eye type, therefore a sensitive/emotional personality type.

Investigation showed chronic reversed polarity, and, as reported by her parents, an extreme sensitivity to sugar. Further exploration into the stress factors surrounding her condition revealed that the trauma of a premature birth was enhanced by the fact that both parents were working two jobs and had moved three times prior to her arrival into the world. Her mother reported a history of nausea and vomiting continually during her pregnancy, and was frequently treated for dehydration in the local emergency room.

It was noted during my intake examination and history that both parents led high-stress lives. The child had been bombarded with these symptoms and emotions during the pregnancy, and after her birth the stressful events continued. It was discovered that the child had adopted the mother's method of vomiting to relieve the stomach, her emotional center.

The standard CRP herbal nutritional program was used. Sugar was removed from the daily diet as much as possible and reserved for special occasions only. Extra hugs and quality individual time with both parents was suggested to meet the needs of her sensitive/emotional personality type.

Results: This child has adjusted well to preschool. All symptoms of her hyperactive behavior have disappeared. She now sleeps normally through the night, her night sweats have stopped, and she no longer vomits. A psychologist who recently examined her commented that she has an "amazing and remarkable vocabulary for a four-year-old."

Discussion: Research indicates that parents who were hyperactive, often with possible neurological or psychological problems, are more prone to having ADD/ADHD disorders in their children. It has also been noted that having one child who is hyperactive increased the risk that siblings will also be affected. Scientists thus conclude a genetic predisposition to this disorder that continues to elude effective treatment by the medical community.

In my experience, chronic reversed polarity is contagious, caused not by germs but by proximity. If you place a live battery next to a dead one, the live battery's charge will be pulled down. Children surrounded by "stressed out" (CRP) parents, or in the uterus of a such a mother, become switched in their polarity as the parents unknowingly pull down the electrical charge of the child. This frequently occurs before birth, often continuing as the child develops on its own without intervention to break the cycle. I predict that research will eventually prove that this creates chemical imbalances in the brain, and ongoing nervous disorders create these symptoms.

Second Case Study

Patient: Male child, seven years old, diagnosed with ADD/ADHD and muscular dystrophy.

History: Muscular dystrophy was discovered after the birth of this child, with accompanying physical limitations. ADHD symptoms were present and severe from the onset. He had problems sitting still, learning, focusing, and following directions. In school, he could not write his name, his spelling lesson was never completed, and he could not do math, even on the simplest level.

Medical treatment: This child is currently receiving ongoing care from a children's hospital, as well as physical therapy. A psychiatrist prescribed Ritalin after a cursory ten-minute examination. This provoked his mom to seek a different, drugless therapy.

Complementary alternative: Investigation and history indicated that this child was the product of an extremely stressful marriage, and difficult delivery. I had previously treated his mother for CRP, and it is notable that she is now divorced and involved in a less stressful relationship. Changes in lifestyle often aid in recovery for both parents and children with CRP.

This child also tested positively for chronic reversed polarity and was given the standard herbal treatment for children to reverse this condition. For this child, who was unable to swallow capsules, the herbs were mixed in apple sauce, juice, a protein drink, or even Ovaltine® to aid digestion. Treatment was continued until the child was not reversed, and minimum doses of the herbal remedies were then maintained to assist in the ongoing healing process.

Results: This young man has had a miraculous year at school. He not only is able to write his name, but he now gets perfect scores on his spelling tests. He was still having difficulty doing math in his head, but was introduced to a new "touch-type" math and is almost caught up to his grade level, which he expects to accomplish this year.

A resource specialist did a battery of IQ tests on this child, called, his mother believes, Woodcock-Johnson tests. The results were scored between 128 and 135 in various categories (superior to very superior range). This child's doctor at the children's hospital calls him "Albert," as in Einstein, who, as we know, was labeled a poor student by his teachers.

This young man's muscular dystrophy appears to be stationary at the time of this writing, and many of the progressive symptoms that generally occur with this disease have not manifested. His physician examines him and remains in awe, frequently telling his mom, "I don't know what you're doing, but keep doing it!" The physical therapist related that this child is becoming a completely different case than any other muscular dystrophy patient he has treated.

Discussion: Genetic counseling revealed that this child's mother did not carry the gene associated with this type of muscular dystrophy. Her physician theorized that due to the stress levels of the mother at conception, she produced a mutated egg, as sometimes happens.

I have found in my own practice that the vast majority of ADHD cases have CRP. Correcting this condition with herbs often produces remarkable results, as in this young man's experience. The intuitive information I have received indicates that muscular dystrophy, cerebral palsy, and many other birth defect conditions are caused by CRP occurring at various stages of the fetus's nervous system development.

Third Case Study

Patient: Fifteen-year-old male high school student with unusual symptoms resistant to confirmed diagnosis.

History: This highly intelligent young man was wasting away. The weight on his 5'8" frame mysteriously dropped to 88 pounds. He was pale, with dark circles under his eyes; his classmates teased him, calling him Dracula. This teen's arms and legs looked like thin sticks, as he had lost most of his muscle mass. His back was becoming stiff, and there was an obvious stoop or curvature to the upper portion. He complained of leg cramps, night sweats, and a tendency to use the wrong words on occasion while speaking. He also exhibited extreme gastrointestinal sensitivity.

Medical treatment: MRI, CAT scan, and other medical testing revealed nothing. The only significant finding was an iron deficiency in the blood analysis. Five separate physicians recommended ferrous sulfate (iron replacement), which only seemed to worsen his condition. The next consideration was the possibility of Crohn's disease, an inflammation of the small bowel that can cause pain and lack of nutrient absorption. Further evaluation, however, ruled this out as well.

Complementary alternative: Upon examination, this young man had all the outward signs of CRP, which was quickly verified. The symptoms seemed closest to ankylosing spondylitis, which is often accompanied by inflammatory bowel diseases such as ulcerative colitis or Crohn's disease. Like most diseases of unknown origin, they are difficult to diagnose until the symptoms are progressed and classic. By this time, it is often too late to stop or reverse the physical damage.

The standard herbal nutritional program for CRP was administered. Due to his gastrointestinal sensitivity, lower-than-normal dosages were initially used.

The majority of imbalances in patients with CRP are not correctable until the polarity is corrected. Therefore, the CRP treatment is continued until normal polarity is achieved. Only then was the mildest iron herb, which also soothed the intestinal tract, used to correct the anemia.

Results: After three months, the patient was halfway out of CRP and had a weight gain of ten pounds. The night sweats and leg cramping had ceased.

Long-term results: The patient has gained 37 pounds. Back stiffness and stooping have resolved completely. Arms and legs have regained muscle mass and appear more normal. Dark circles under the eyes have dissipated and the pale skin tone is gone. He has recently graduated from high school and has accomplished some special computer design work. I am told that he has recently completed a spy novel, as yet unpublished. In every way, this special genius child is back to a *normal* life, if "normal" is indeed applicable to such a capable young man!

Discussion: In this case, with such severe physical symptoms and such high intelligence, the patient was not taken to a psychiatrist, so hyperactivity and/or ADD was not considered. However, if he had been correctly evaluated, he could have been diagnosed as ADHD.

In my practice, I have learned that stress is a major cause of CRP. As I got to know this young man, I found a well-intended family with stress of a spiritual nature. This student was also a superachiever intellectually. Several scholastic achievements had so stressed this young man that his polarity had reversed and his disease process began.

I believe this case typifies the possible extreme problems of Indigo Children. Hyperactivity medications would not have been a solution, nor would prednisone or other anti-inflammatory drugs have helped this condition.

In Summary

Lumping people into a "blanket" diagnosis, such as ADD or ADHD, and recommending immediate drug therapy is not the answer. With both ADHD and depression, studies are now showing that more serious conditions often occur later. The mainstream system does not work, especially for our special Indigo Children! The research continues, and much headway and greater understanding is beginning within the medical community. They are, however, only beginning to understand the vastness of the problems caused by today's stressful world. The perfect solutions are yet to come.

Every parent should learn about the options available in understanding these children. We cannot have healthy, happy, balanced children when we ourselves are out of balance, full of stress or hopelessness, or suffering from chronic reversed polarity. Many parents of Indigo Children find that, as they assist their children, they also heal themselves.

Major research concludes that no current treatment, intervention, or approach works on ADD, ADHD, or LD-diagnosed children. Another study from Yale University concludes that 74 percent of children whose learning disabilities were discovered in third grade remain disabled in ninth grade, and another study shows that Ritalin usage has doubled between 1990 and 1995 to 1.5 million children.[70] This figure could be approaching 2.5 million by the time of this writing.

Drug therapy is primarily being used to make these children more *manageable*, not to cure them. In another study, men treated for ADHD in childhood exhibited three times the incidence of drug abuse as the control group.[70] Several studies indicate an unusually high percentage of prison inmates were treated for ADD/ADHD disorders as children. These figures are alarming, as more and more children are entering our world with greater stress factors than ever before.

I recommend investigating alternatives for these beautiful children. Drug therapy may help with the presenting symptoms but seldom heals the root cause. Research is ongoing as scientists search for better methods of treatment. In many cases, the entire family needs to be evaluated and the stress factors understood. Only then can we hope to create a healthy environment for these sensitive souls to flourish.

There is so much more to be discovered about ourselves and our children as we move into this new time. There are many, like myself, who will serve these children. They cannot continue to be placed under a blanket classification and treated alike. Each is very different and needs to be treated and understood accordingly. It's up to you. You may choose to accept mainstream therapy as the best of a bad group of choices, or you can seek other methods to find what *does* work for your child and your family.

Parents and friends of Indigo Children: Consider well the individual needs of these new teachers. You must be special role models. Honor their individuality. Seek truth and alternatives to the status quo. Above all, never give up!

We told you that we research these things before we present them—and the best research is real stories about real children. Shortly after we received the above submission, we got the following letter from **Bella Richards** about her daughter, Norine. We wanted to share it with you:

> My daughter is 15 years old and presently being treated by Keith Smith, iridologist and herbalist in Escondido, California. We believe she is an Indigo Child, and under Keith's treatment she has shown remarkable improvement. She is in her second year in high school and was having a very

hard time, showing signs of ADD, and not able to concentrate
or stay focused in school. We went to both her doctor and a
neurologist, but neither could find anything wrong with her.

I was really feeling discouraged as this poor girl failed the
tenth grade. I just wanted to take her out of regular school and
put her in continuation school. I argued intensely with the vice
principal, and desperately tried to find out what was wrong
with her. She is extremely bright and wise, but she has a really hard time relating to her peers. She just seems to be a misfit for her day and age.

When we finally took this poor child to Keith, he knew
exactly what her problem was just by looking at her and listening to what she told him. It has been a real blessing. I can't
explain how frustrating it is when no one can relate!

We cannot leave nutritional supplements out of the solution
for Indigo or even ADD kids. What follows, however, is far
beyond mere nutrition. Can nutrition be a substitute for Ritalin?
This might be comical, but here are two quotes with opposing
views, both from very good sources:

*"'It's a fixed, stable, low-dose drug.' Critics who claim diet,
exercise or other treatments work just as well as Ritalin
are kidding themselves."*[1]
—Dr. Philip Berent, consulting psychiatrist at the Arlington
Center for Attention Deficit Disorder in Arlington Heights, IL

*"There has been intriguing work to suggest that at least some chil-
dren with ADHD may respond to nutritional treatments, including
the addition of certain fatty oils, or the elimination of other foods
from their diet . . . . more research is needed."*[1]
— The National Institutes of Health, 1998

Does this suggest to you that the jury is still out? Don't be badgered into thinking that nutrition doesn't matter. It does! The next three submissions are about nutritional supplements that have had a profound effect on ADD children and Indigos.

Karen Eck is from Oregon. Besides being an independent educational consultant and a distributor for educational software, she has spent her life on a quest for healing without drugs. This has led her right into nutrition, among other things. At present, Karen works with a company called Insight USA,[74] who make *Smart Start,* a nutritional supplement. They are having good results with adults, as well as many children with ADD (and also Indigos misdiagnosed with ADD). We are not here to promote products or companies, but sometimes that's the only way to obtain the results of careful research into exactly what we need. If you know of other companies with other health products positively known to help with Indigo or ADD children, then write us. We will definitely check it out and put it on our Indigo website at **www.Indigochild.com.**

A Nutritional Answer
Karen Eck

The story of *Smart Start* is about building blocks. Your child began playing with simple combinations of building blocks and eventually learned to build complex, functional toys. In the same way, your body starts with simple building blocks and is able to build complex functional body systems, including the learning centers of the brain.

We should get these nutritional building blocks from the food we eat. Unfortunately, many of the essential nutritional building blocks are refined out of our diets, leaving us with a body that sometimes lacks the full spectrum of nutrients that add individuality and creativity to our lives. So, when *Smart Start* was developed, the cornerstone concept was to make sure it contained the essential building blocks of nutrition. Researchers have focused the aim of *Smart Start* on mental performance.

Trace minerals are usually missing from refined foods, yet they are the foundation of most enzymes in the body. Enzymes speed up body functions ranging from sight to nerve impulses. The minerals in the *Smart Start* products, so unique that they are patented by Albion Laboratories, are chelated to be readily absorbed by the body. This means that your body doesn't have to work so hard to absorb its nutritional building blocks.

Vitamins are, by their very definition, building blocks of nutrition that your body cannot make itself. These must be replenished daily to energize and protect it.

The other components are equally vital for optimum well-being. Lecithin, for example, makes up 75 percent of your brain. Other building blocks are not so easy to see, but often are most important.

Ginkgo biloba, for instance, is a common shade tree, native to China, with bitter-tasting flavonoids that increase blood flow to the brain as well as stabilizing the blood-brain barrier. This barrier is the most discriminating filter in the body. It regulates the amount of energy-producing sugars and oxygen the brain receives, as well as protecting it from harmful substances.

Studies have shown that antioxidants such as pycnogenol, a pine bark extract, improve one's eyesight. Herbs are well known for improving longevity, and together with vitamins and trace minerals, give *Smart Start* a full spectrum of nutritional building blocks.

Smart Start is a unique dietary supplement formulated with emphasis on important trace nutrients needed to support optimal learning performance. These ingredients have been called "smart nutrients."

This supplement combines important chelated minerals, antioxidant vitamins, and botanicals in a great-tasting chewable tablet that is ideal for children. However, it's not just "kids' stuff"—it's for every member of the family.

Each bottle contains 90 tablets, a one-month supply.

Components of *Smart Start:*

Each 3 tablets contain:	Amount:	% US RDI:
Vitamin A (beta carotene)	5,000 IU	100
Vitamin C (ascorbic acid)	60 mg	100
Vitamin D (cholecalciferol)	400 IU	100
Vitamin E (min. tocopherols)	30 IU	100
Vitamin B$_1$ (thiamin mononitrate)	1.5 mg	100
Vitamin B$_2$ (riboflavin)	2.0 mg	100
Vitamin B$_6$ (cyanocobalamin)	6 mcg	100
Vitamin B$_{12}$ (pyridoxine HCL)	200 mcg	100
Folic acid	400 mcg	100
Biotin	300 mcg	100
Niacinamide	20 mcg	100
Pantothenic acid (d-calcium pantothenate)	10 mcg	100
Iron*	4.5 mg	25
Zinc*	3.75 mg	25
Manganese*	1 mg	–
Copper*	0.5 mg	25
Chromium*	410 mcg	–
Lecithin	80 mcg	–
Iodine (potassium iodide)	37.5 mcg	25
Molybdenum*	18 mcg	25
Selenium*	10 mcg	–

The six minerals starred above are Albion Laboratories' patented brand of amino acid chelate, which also contains a unique proprietary blend of the following herbs that have been associated with mental function:

Gingko biloba leaf	40 mg
Bilberry (anthocynanadin concentrate)	20 mg
Kelp plant	12 mg
Black walnut hull	12 mg
Siberian ginseng root	12 mg
Pycnogenol	400 mg

Also contains: fructose, dextrose, glycine, citric acid, flavor, and stearic acid.

As you can see, the components of Smart Start are many and varied. They have a wide range of benefits, as described in the following three sections.

Vitamins

Vitamins are often depleted from the foods we eat, especially fried foods. Since vitamins cannot be manufactured by our bodies, they must be supplied by the food and supplements we consume. They are most important to our energy production, stress responses, and immunity.

Beta carotene (vitamin A): Antioxidant (not stored by the liver; relatively nontoxic)

Vitamins C and E: Antioxidant

Vitamin D: Required for calcium absorption

Vitamins B_1, B_2, B_6, B_{12}, and Niacinamide: Each required for energy production and stress response

Folic acid: Required for energy production

Biotin: Essential growth factor for all cells in the body

Pantothenic acid: Strengthens immune response

Trace Minerals

Since trace minerals are removed from many of the foods we eat, Smart Start gives trace minerals a prominent place in its formulation. Trace minerals are the catalysts for hundreds of enzyme reactions in the body. These reactions control nearly all bodily functions from nerve impulses to blood sugar levels. All these actions are critical to life and learning.

Iron and molybdenum: Component of red blood cells

Zinc: Component of over 60 enzymes, including those essential for manufacturing the body's natural antioxidants

Manganese: Essential to enzymes required for bone growth, energy production, and immunity

Copper: Particularly important for enzymes relating to immunity and cardiovascular health

Chromium: Essential for healthy sugar and fat metabolism

Iodine: Essential to produce thyroid enzymes

Selenium: Component of essential immunity enzymes

Herbal Components

The herbs in Smart Start are designed to maximize one's natural ability to learn.

Ginkgo biloba: Contains bitter-tasting compounds that stabilize the blood-brain barrier and keep unwanted substances out of the brain

Bilberry: Provides proanthocynadins (antioxidants) that protect individual cells

Black walnut: Natural source of iodine (metabolic balancer; provides energy to the body)

Siberian ginseng: Contains adaptogens that improve one's response to stress

Pycnogenol: Antioxidant extracted from pine bark

Lecithin: The brain is composed primarily of phospholipids (lecithin-like compounds)

Summary

After using *Smart Start*, parents have made comments such as, "It's as if somebody's home now, and the lights *are* on!" One parent went on vacation without the nutritionals and sorely missed them, as the child's behavior again became erratic. Many times the parents will run out and not notice what a big change there has been until they are missing; they are soon making panicked phone calls to replenish their supply!

Our interactive educational software is also making huge differences in the lives of ADD and ADHD children. The children enjoy one-on-one attention with the computer, which also gives them instant feedback. One child would often do his lessons standing up and squirming around, but he loved getting the answers correct. It was wonderful to see. These children then become aware that they are smart and can learn. Self-esteem soars! Behavior problems decline.

Deborah Grossman is the mother of an Indigo Child, a homeopathist, and an R.N. She has developed a nutritional supplement schedule that works, and she wishes to share it. Note that within the given list there is something called **blue-green algae.** This is perhaps one of the biggest surprises of all, and is discussed right after we hear from Deborah.

Protocol for Supplementing Your ADHD Child
Deborah Grossman, R.N.

I have no doubt that my son *chose* me because he knew that I would not let him get "chewed up and spit out" as the old paradigm dissolves. I have been involved in holistic medicine for years and am used to dealing with crumbling systems. The one I am currently trying to influence is the educational system. My perception is that these Indigo Children are operating at a level where it is often hard for them to deal with tedious tasks, particularly those that deal with pen, paper, and boring memorization.

The protocol that I use with my son includes the blue-green algae from Klamath Lake, with some additions. This protocol has been developed using my son as the proverbial guinea pig; I find that certain things work very well together. This is a daily dosage:

- Source of Life multivitamin
- (3) Super Choline capsules
- (2) 5-H-T-P capsules by Biochem
- (1) 1,000 mg capsule of lecithin
- (1) 50 mg lipoic acid capsule by Biochem

- (1) Capsule Rhododendron Caucasicum+ (often obtainable only by mail order)
- (3) Restores (a mail-order compilation of amino acids)
- (2) capsules of Omega Gold (a mail-order blue-green algae combo)
- (1) DHA Capsule by Solray
- (2) Efalex Focus Capsules
- Trace Lyte added to reverse-osmosis water

I am fortunate that my son cooperates in taking this long list of supplements. My son weighs about 105 pounds, so adjust your dosage accordingly. For children who cannot take pills, there is a spray called Pedi Active that can be used for the first couple of supplements.

A Canadian company called Nutrichem[75] carries products that contain most of the ingredients in my formulation, with fewer pills because there is no filler. The cost may also be less.

Alternative Choices

We would like to present some alternate methods of health and balance that may seem odd—but they work. We mentioned earlier that today's weirdness is often tomorrow's science. It's true. With the increasing popularity and validation of many alternate healing methods, medical science is finally getting around to looking at the strange and weird with a new eye. The new thinking seems to be, *If it works, there may be something to it. We'll find out later why it works.* This is a vast improvement over the old days when the thinking was, *It can't possibly work, since we don't know why.* Some ideas that were actually branded as "silly" in our culture just a few years ago are today being prescribed by the very people who called it that.

Alternate and complementary medical wings are springing up in hospitals all over America, with many people being helped by heretofore unsubstantiated methods of balance and healing. For many professionals, the methods are indeed still unsubstantiated—but working. Acupuncture is now on some HMO insurance plans, finally being recognizing as another culture's very old science that has merit—one that was poo-poohed by established medicine for decades.

Even some very ancient remedies that seemed really bizarre are now being brought into real science. Listen to a report from the Associated Press, November 1998:[76]

> It's an ancient Chinese remedy that many U.S. doctors will find bizarre: heating the herb mugwort next to the little toe of a pregnant woman to help turn her baby out of the risky breech position just before birth.
>
> But when thousands of doctors this week open the *Journal of the American Medical Association,* they'll find a scientific study that says the Chinese therapy really works and Western women should try it.

According to a 1997 study in the *New England Journal of Medicine,* a remarkable 46 percent of Americans have used an alternative medical treatment such as acupuncture or chiropractic therapy. According to the same report, in a list of most commonly used alternatives, "spiritual healing by others" ranked as number five![76]

Take a look at what follows. There may be something here for you!

The Lake Klamath Miracle: Blue-Green Algae

We recommended Edward Hallowell's book on ADD early in this chapter. He is a leading authority in learning disabilities, particularly ADD. He has written a *New York Times* bestseller, *Driven to Distraction.*[58] As mentioned, it is considered the most comprehensive book on the subject of ADD and ADHD children.

Dr. Hallowell was the keynote speaker at the 1998 Pacific Region Learning Disabilities Drug Treatment Conference in Honolulu, Hawaii, where a portion of his address involved non-drug treatments for ADD. At the top of his list was blue-green algae, a wild food that is harvested from Upper Klamath Lake in southern Oregon by a company called Cell Tech.

The Klamath Lake blue-green algae is being touted as a "superfood" because of the effects it is having on so many who have discovered it. It's a natural food that is harvested rather than manufactured, and is unlikely to be laced with preservatives, artificial dyes, or flavor modifiers.

Another industry psychologist, John F. Taylor, is author of *Helping your Hyperactive ADD Child*[59] and the video *Answers to ADD: The School Success Tool Kit.*[77] He is quoted in the nutrition edition of *Network of Hope* newsletter:

> While having no connection with any company involved in harvest, manufacture or marketing of foods, medicines, or nutrients, I have been in a position to talk with thousands of parents and professionals very frankly about ADD and ADHD, and blue-green algae is consistently mentioned to me by parents as being of help for children with ADD and ADHD.[78]

Remember that not all ADD children are Indigo, but many Indigos seem to have some of the same apparent attributes, sometimes brought on by what they are forced to endure in the non-Indigo-accepting family and structure around them. Therefore, we have discovered that many parents of Indigo Children are very successfully using blue-green algae from Klamath Lake as a nutritional supplement—and swearing by it! They tell us that it stabilizes blood sugar, is free from toxins, contains critical vitamins (especially a concentrated source of beta-carotene and vitamin B_{12}), and has other characteristics of "superfoods."

Of all the substances we have heard of in our travels, this one sticks out as the most mentioned, and the most effective by itself. Can it help with ADD? Will it help balance Indigo attributes? There are those who really think so—and the proof seems to be everywhere. Many feel it should be included in everyone's diet!

If you want to try it, contact Cell Tech.[79] If you would like to read three scientific studies on blue-green algae regarding children, you are invited to view **www.the-peoples.net/celltech.**

Following are several systems and methods that are working with ADD children (and some Indigos). While not mainstream, credible people and validating studies stand behind them.

The Magnetic Connection

It is our opinion that the connection between magnetics and the human body are profound. This is due to our very close connection to several researchers that do magnetic healing work. Most of this work is leading-edge in the areas of cancer and disease control, so it doesn't quite fit into this book. In addition, some of the work is in the genesis stage and can't be validated yet, despite the really outstanding laboratory results that we know about. We were about. We were going to skip it until we got a synchronistic letter from **Patti McCann-Para,** showing that there are other medical doctors who are having results specifically with ADD and magnets. Patti states in her letter:

> I just finished a book that mentions the use of static magnets in children with attention problems. It's titled *Magnetic Therapy,* by Ron Lawrence, M.D., Ph.D.; Paul Rosch, M.D., F.A.C.P.; and Judith Plowden.[80] In chapter 8 on page 167, they tell of Dr. Bernard Margolis of Harrisburg, PA, who is having wonderful success with static magnets in these children. He speaks of self-esteem issues and the like, as well. Dr. Margolis told of a simple study with 28 children, ages 5 to 18, where all but two patients were male. He told of a study at the Conference of The North American Academy of Magnetic Therapy held in Los Angeles in 1998. Dr. Margolis used static (or permanent) magnets in his study, and the judges of the effects of the magnet therapy were the best ones: the parents of the kids! Parents reported that magnets helped their children immeasurably. Some said that "it was like night and day. [The child] was lovable with the magnetic therapy, and without . . . was up for adoption."

We can't move out of this area until we give you general advice from those who are studying magnetics and the human body, although this has nothing to do with Indigo Children specifically: Please, please don't use magnetic mattresses or chairs for months and months as personal healing/feel-good devices. This practice exposes your body to a constant potential that can change your cellular instruction sets. Use the devices on and off—not permanently! We believe that eventually there will be research to show the detrimental effects. If permanent magnet therapy can heal people when used carefully, delicately, and expertly, think about what an array of hundreds of them, used crudely and ignorantly, could do.

Biofeedback and Neurotherapy

If you were interested in the HeartMath® system[49] we spoke of in chapter 2, then what follows in this short discussion of biofeedback will sound similar. We spoke then of brain measurements that showed chaos or joy, anger or love, and a system to help humans balance behavior. Here is a more medical approach—one that has been around awhile, but should not be overlooked.

Donna King is a certified neurotherapy provider and an associate fellow from the Biofeedback Certification Institute of America. She is the professional education director for the Behavioral Physiology Institutes,[81] a graduate school in behavioral medicine in Washington state. She wrote a brief but compelling note about her findings:

> I am writing because I have had the great pleasure to work with many children who have been diagnosed with ADD or ADHD. I use an electroencephalograph (EEG) to measure their brain waves, then teach the child to change their own brain waves until they feel they can function comfortably. These kids are able to reduce or eliminate their medication. Sleep improves, bed-wetting stops, and outbursts of anger disappear. This method of treatment, EEG Neuro-feedback or EEG Biofeedback, empowers children and allows them to choose their behavior, rather than being forced into it through either drugs or the need to conform.[82]

Biofeedback and neurotherapy aren't new or strange. In fact, Donna provided many pages of documentation regarding the intense studies of why this works, as well as some studies regarding children in general.[83] As she mentioned, she works with children daily, and is very vocal about how much help they can receive. This is accredited science, and it is working with many children!

There are probably dozens of neurofeedback and neurotherapy organizations and disciplines that we are not showing you. Here is another that appeared synchronistically with Donna's input. An organization called The Focus Neuro-Feedback Training Center has arisen with specific emphasis on ADD and ADHD.[84] Norbert Goigelman, Ph.D., founded the Focus Center, which involves the study of Neuronal Regulation (SSNR), and is certified in neurofeedback. He has a doctorate degree in electronic engineering as well as a Ph.D. in psychology, and specializes in providing help for those with ADD and ADHD using neurofeedback.

Here is what his training center had to say:

> With today's sophisticated computers, ADD and ADHD sufferers are provided with a wonderful *non-drug alternative.* EEG neurofeedback is a safe, non-invasive, painless training procedure in which the individual (6 years or older) gets EEG sensors placed on his/her scalp.
>
> These sensors provide information to a computer about the person's brain wave activity. The information is displayed on a color monitor screen. As people see this representation of their own brain's activity, they become conscious of their patterns and can learn to change. Progress is rewarded through visual and auditory feedback.
>
> EEG Neuro-Feedback Training has been likened to a video game in which the rewards are increased performance at school or work, enhanced self-esteem, and realization of untapped potential. After the initial course of training, people rarely need further consultations, training, or medication.

Neuromuscular Integration

How about a system that deals with the brain just as neuro-feedback did, but also integrates the body structure into a system of healing? **Karen Bolesky, M.A., C.M.H.C., L.M.P.,** is a certified medical health counselor. She has been trained in psychotherapy, and is a practitioner and teacher for the Soma Institute of Neuromuscular Integration.[85] She is also its co-director.

This system, like the others, is currently being used with ADD and ADHD children successfully. Soma Neuromuscular Integration is a type of bodymind therapy that changes people physically and psychologically. This change is a result of structurally balancing the body while simultaneously working with the nervous system. The technique consists of ten basic sessions that use deep tissue manipulation, movement training, dialogue between client and practitioner, journaling, and other learning tools to progressively realign the entire body and recondition the nervous system.

Sounds like a tall order! The Soma system is similar to other systems available, but it is one of the few we have seen that combines myofascial work with neurological therapy. For general healing, both Jan and I have experienced the work of our friend Dr. Sid Wolf[86] (who works with a contributor in this book, Dr. Melanie Melvin). He focuses purely on myofascial release, and gets very positive and immediate results! That's one of the reasons we decided to look into Soma for you—it seemed to extend Dr. Wolf's very successful work.

The Soma system was developed by Bill Williams, Ph.D. His team calls the system a "three-brain model," which is simply a metaphor that describes how it works. According to Karen Bolesky, "The Soma goal in working with a client using the three-brain model is to create an environment in which the client begins to experience and have volition over which 'brain' is more effective in the present moment or present task." She explains that it may be more effective to access another "brain" besides the more dominant left hemisphere. Soma, in theory as well as in practical application, is designed to reintegrate the three brains so that one can function more optimally, and experience greater wellness, wholeness, and aliveness, according to Karen.

Regarding ADD and ADHD in particular, she reports:

> All clients diagnosed with ADD or ADHD . . . show left hemisphere dominance to such a degree that it becomes aberrated into overdominance. This keeps the client in the survival mode of the left hemisphere. In survival mode people are fearful of letting go of the left hemisphere; therefore they feel great overwhelm of the concentration span, which is limited to sixteen bits per second. Stated in Soma terms: their sixteen bits are full! Soma works with each client to find ways to access all three "brains," thus allowing more personal ease and expansion. I consider ADD and ADHD more of a state of "fixation in the left hemisphere dominance" than a condition. The Soma bodywork is very effective in expanding the internal experience of the person to a more integrated state. Integration allows greater energy exchange between body and mind, which releases the state of overwhelm.

Soma Work: A Case Study
by Karen Bolesky

A very bright eight-year-old boy, referred by his primary physician, had a full psychological profile and was diagnosed as having ADD. The child had been seen by school counselors and private counselors. His family brought him to me, stressed by his behavior at home and school. They were at wit's end and felt Soma was "a last resort." He would not follow directions, work quietly, demonstrate good manners, complete his homework, maintain neatness, or accept responsibility for his behavior. Most difficult was his aggressive behavior at school and constant arguing with siblings at home.

He played lots of Nintendo™ and computer games, which are very results-oriented, left-hemisphere actions. He hated to be wrong and liked to be alone when nervous. In school, most of his aggression was over the use of the computer. He told me that when he felt stressed, he wanted to play on the computer. He had good mental awareness of his body but felt uncomfortable in it most of the time. He stated that his "brain is nervous, stomach mixed up, hands angry, knees nervous, eyes nervous, and spine mixed up." This informed me that he had a keen inner awareness of his body, and it wasn't difficult to see why he didn't want to continually be conscious of those feelings.

I did four weekly sessions on him with progressive results. The first session was difficult to perform or achieve results from, due to his short attention span. However, he immediately and positively responded to the Soma work. It was difficult to bring his awareness into his body. He wanted to giggle, resist, and distract himself in any way from his "feeling self." I let him guide me. Due to his short attention span, I had to work efficiently. I asked him to stop me if the work was too invasive. This demanded that he pay attention and allow himself a sense of control. After just one session, he proudly announced that he'd had "no fights that week."

After the fourth session, he informed me that he didn't want to do any more bodywork. He said "I've gotten so much better since I've started that I don't need any more. I'll get better by myself now." I believed him. He has never demonstrated aggressive behavior since session one. He is doing well in school and at home and has even become an avid soccer player.

My assessment is that when he surrendered control of the left hemisphere and felt his corebrain (the part of the three-brain model that governs where we experience bodily sensation and energy), he was reminded that this body was a safe place. In the corebrain, he felt his body's energy, which reduced his feeling of being overwhelmed. He then began the process of integration, allowing him a greater expanse of energy with less effort. Health returned when he reclaimed his core. It has been 19 months since his sessions ended.

In summary: If my theory is correct and ADD and ADHD result from a fixed dominance in the left hemisphere, then greater integration will allow a more expanded attention span with greater ease. Most children diagnosed with ADD or ADHD who have gone through the Soma sessions have improved somewhat, usually showing noticeable behavior changes. They are able to cope more effortlessly and show greater ease in focusing their attention.

Rapid Eye Technology

Ranae Johnson, Ph.D., is the founder of the Rapid Eye Institute in Oregon, and the author of two books, *Rapid Eye*

Technology and *Winter's Flower.*[87] The Rapid Eye technique was actually developed out of trying to find alternate treatments for autism! *Winter's Flower* is the heartwarming story of how it all happened as Ranae tried to find help for her autistic son. In the process, she found methods to help not only him, but also ADD and ADHD children and adults. Here are some thoughts from the organization:

Rapid Eye Technology (RET) addresses the physical, emotional, mental, and spiritual aspects of the being. At the physical level, one learns to access the stressful information stored in the body and release stress at the cellular level. The body learns a new skill for consciously releasing stress, which can then help with all stressful incidents in life. The body's natural healthy state can then balance the biochemistry and create health.

At the emotional level, RET facilitates the release of negative emotional energy (negative energy is associated with disease). Clients learn how to release negative energy or use it positively to create different results in their lives.

At the mental level, practitioners educate clients using the life skills. The life skills are spiritual principles that assist the client in achieving a different perspective on life. It has been said that if you always do what you have always done, you will always get what you have always gotten. The cognitive portion of RET gives clients a way to do things differently than they have ever done them in the past. The client can access these spiritual principles and realize their self-empowerment in the creation of life.

At the spiritual level, Rapid Eye Technology reminds people of their perfection. The release of stress opens clients to their spiritual nature. This allows them to determine their sense of purpose in life and avoid the "existential vacuum" that can result in dis-ease.

Rapid Eye Technology accesses the limbic system through the eyes and the ears. The limbic system is the part of the brain responsible for processing emotions. The eyes are connected to the limbic system through a part of the body called the lateral geniculate nuclei, and the ears are connected to the limbic system through the medial geniculate nuclei. This connection makes it possible for the client to process stress at the cellular level through the pituitary gland, which regulates the biochemical cellular functions of the body. Through the hippocampus (another part of the limbic system) and other related memory areas of the brain, the client has the ability to access and release stress related to past events.

As we were evaluating many processes for this book, we received a letter from the training team at the Rapid Eye Institute.[88] They collectively said:

> Having 12 children between us, ages 6 to 30, we definitely feel we have our share of what you describe as Indigo Children. We have directly experienced ADD, ADHD, autism and other labels. We teach a way of approaching parenting based on the Universal principles (Life Skills program), with wonderful results.

From the founder:

> The Rapid Eye techniques and our Life Skills program have assisted my children and grandchildren, along with all the thousands of other technicians that have come for training, and all their clients, to magnify their journeys and move into co-creating their lives. It is so exciting to witness many alternative healing modalities coming together with our medical model to form an eclectic holistic form of healing.

The EMF Balancing Technique

The EMF Balancing Technique® is one of the newest (and perhaps most open to eye-rolling) techniques to come along in metaphysical circles. It looks very much like "hands-on" healing, but it has had such a startling rate of results that even NASA wanted to study it at one time! If you want to know more about this technique that's "not fully explainable, but working," then take a look. **Peggy and Steve Dubro** have developed it, and they are working around the world to train others in its use.[89] From their website:

> The EMF Balancing Technique is the energy system designed to work with the *Universal Calibration Lattice*, a model of the human energy anatomy. It is a simple, systematic procedure anyone can learn. The system utilizes the human-to-human effect upon the electromagnetic field. . . . [It integrates] spirit (God-self) and biology. There are four phases, each designed to strengthen the EMF patterns needed to successfully co-create your reality in the new energy.

The NASA interest? Evidently a company that's called Sonalysts proposed for a grant to study this work. The EMF part of the experiment was to provide training and exercises to test the effect of electromagnetic field energy awareness on "improving team performance" and "strengthening the human health maintenance process," or in other words, to stimulate collective consciousness by integrating spirit and biology!

Our advice? Go ahead and roll your eyes, then send your Indigos—they won't.

chapter five

Messages from Indigos

In this chapter, we get to actually hear from some Indigos who are now grown, or almost grown. One of the difficult things about finding some older Indigos to write for us was that the Indigo label is brand new. If it were not for a small chapter on the Indigo experience that I included in my last book, *Partnering with God,* we would not have these stories at all. We received them last year, mostly due to that small mention. Once this book is released, however, there will be many who realize that either they are Indigo, or they have Indigo Children, relatives, or friends. We know this because of the thousands who attend our seminars throughout the world who've heard this message and are startled by how relevant it is to what is happening in their lives.

Ryan Maluski is in his early to mid-20s. Indigos of this age are usually the forerunners, the first to arrive. We can almost guarantee that they have been diagnosed with problems—although ADD was not yet the much-used diagnosis it is today, they probably were labeled with mental disorders or anything else that might connote "misfit." Also, many older Indigos mention spiritual aspects.

It seems to come with the territory. As you read Ryan's account, try to identify some of the Indigo traits that you have learned in this book.

Growing Up Indigo
Ryan Maluski

Describing my feelings growing up as an Indigo is not an easy task because there is just so much to tell. Also, I do not know what it is like *not* growing up Indigo, so you see my dilemma. Let me begin by saying this: I always knew I belonged here on Earth, and I always had a deep-seated universal knowledge of how things really work and who I really was. Yet, with grand humor, I chose to grow up with people in situations and places that reflected absolutely none of my sense of self. Can you begin to see the infinite possibilities for fun in this play I chose to come into? I was very challenged; I felt very different and alone. I felt surrounded by aliens who, having invaded my home, tried to mold me into what they felt I should be. To put it bluntly, I felt like a king working for a peasant, viewed as a slave.

I grew up in a middle-class Catholic family in the suburbs of Westchester County, New York. I chose to be blessed with two loving parents and a sister five years younger. In my infancy, I sometimes reached very high fevers, went into convulsions, and was taken to the hospital and put on ice. I was medicated for about two years with Phenobarbitol to assist in controlling the convulsions. My mother noticed that I easily became sicker around large groups of people, so she kept me away from crowds whenever possible. Her friends and relatives never understood, and they criticized her, but she knew that she had to do this.

My parents gave me everything within their scope. I was given much attention and showered with love. I was taken to a petting zoo almost daily. I remember the animals there; I felt they were mine. I even let the goats out of their area into the park, which was very amusing to me. My first time at the circus was interesting, and my mother tells this story:

> Ryan was two when we were at the three-ring circus. He had his own seat, but I was so excited and didn't want him to miss anything, so I put him on my lap. And as he watched happily, I was so excited that I kept saying, "Ryan, look at this! Ryan, look at that! Ryan, see the clowns and elephants!" And all of a sudden, he turned around and slapped me across the face! Then he turned back to watch the circus. The doctor said I overstimulated him and to just leave him alone, let him enjoy, and take things in on his own.

When I was about seven, I noticed that I did some things differently. For instance, if I went to a candy store and was told to pick out the candy I wanted, I would only pick what I wanted at that moment. I wouldn't totally raid the place. The cashier remarked how different that was. Most children would hoard all that they could, but I only took the small amount that I felt I needed or wanted at that time.

For Christmas, I had lots of presents, but when I opened the first one, I would sit there and play with it for a while, until my mother encouraged me to move on to the next gift. I was simply grateful for that one gift, and really in the moment, locked onto that one present. I would stay focused on that present all day.

When I was younger, I was often able to stare at an object and feel my whole being kind of move toward it—almost leaving my body—and I would be able to see it from every angle, and every single sense was dramatically heightened, and everything felt larger. I would tell my friends, and they would have absolutely no idea what I was talking about. I felt weird, misunderstood, and "wrong."

High school was the most challenging and painful time of my life, when kids compare themselves and fitting in and feeling accepted are most important. Any type of weirdness stuck out like a sore thumb. I definitely felt weird. Early on, I had many friends and got along with every type of group, but as time passed I felt myself drift away from everyone else. I was in a world of my own; it was very lonely. This enraged me. All I wanted to be was "normal."

Around age 15, I told my parents how I was feeling—depressed, paranoid, and different. I had anxiety attacks and acted out weird, obsessive-compulsive rituals that made no logical sense, but that I needed to do to feel safe. I also heard degrading, negative, and manipulative voices in my mind. My mind and emotions would race. It was difficult to hold any kind of focus for long. It was difficult to control myself—I felt like a coiled-up spring. I felt that I was 10,000 volts of energy in a body that could hold only half that. I was like a live wire with no grounding cord. I had mild tics—Tourette's syndrome. My parents took me to doctors—many doctors.

I balanced my inner chaos with humor, becoming the class clown. I would gladly receive detention to get some attention. It was very important for me to do anything I could to make people laugh. When I did this, I was actually interacting with them on the planet—I was noticed!

Then there were times when I could just sit by myself and think of an entire scenario in my mind—a sort of play where I could act out any characters I chose, doing whatever I wanted. Sometimes I just suddenly started laughing hysterically, and when asked why, my explanation made absolutely no sense to others.

Being funny helped me forget my "stuff"—laughing feels so good. However, I was also very unpredictable, switching moods instantly and without warning. I was called psycho, loony, and so on—and I believed it. That's how I really felt. I thought I would never escape the prison I was in. Various medications helped me with certain challenges for a certain period of time, but after a while, something else would pop up. When I was about 15, one of the top doctors in the world specializing in Tourette's syndrome told me and my parents that I was the most unique case he had ever had: "It seems when we fix one thing, something else comes up. He has all these little cubbyholes of problems. I have never been so baffled in my life."

At the time, I even felt proud that I couldn't be figured out, because that meant there was still hope. Medication did not take away or control all the pain and confusion, but I discovered that alcohol did. I would take to my room in privacy almost daily and drink away all problems. Drinking would numb me and put me in a safe, secure, familiar, and always accessible world. Cigarettes were also a way to fit in and at least feel a little bit normal.

At about 16, I was hyperactive and started a new medication. One evening I was so jumpy that my mother and I called the doctor, who said to take another pill to calm down. So I took it and became twice as jumpy. Then I called another doctor for confirmation, and she told me that the pills themselves were making me feel this way. I was ready to jump out of my skin, and I begged my mother to buy me alcohol to numb it. It was unbearable; dying was a pleasant thought, as it would end this hell. I felt locked in my body.

By my senior year of high school, I was desperate, so I volunteered to go into a psychiatric hospital. My therapist recommended this, and I agreed, with no idea what I was doing. I was with about 25 other children between the ages of 10 and 18. I actually felt pretty well off in there, seeing the array of challenges and problems everyone else had. This first time, I stayed about a month. After a few days, I noticed how almost all the other children would come talk to me when they were upset. They all opened up to me and would take any advice I gave them. The hospital staff wasn't too fond of this, wondering how I, another "crazy patient," could help anyone. They mirrored my inner self-created prison. Now it was real and frightening.

One night, the reality of where I was hit me, and I broke down in my room, crying, "Why me?" over and over. On my first day, I witnessed four restraints, where the staff took patients who were out of control, wrestled them to the ground, injected them with Thorazine, and strapped them onto a bed in the quiet room until they calmed down. Then it was probation—no phone calls, no visitors, no TV, no leaving your room, and "leave the door open" so a staff member can watch you around the clock. I loved my freedom, so I made sure this never happened to me.

The frustrating part of all the hospital's rules was that they were enforced by people who I could clearly see had many problems themselves! I could see this, being gifted with the ability to "read" people. My family and friends from school would visit me, lending great support. I spent my 18th birthday in the hospital, and I even missed my senior prom. I did not feel like a man. I had plenty of reasons to feel sorry for myself. I remember saying, "I will overcome all of this and then show all the other children how to do the same. I know there is a way."

When I graduated from high school and chose not to go to college, my parents clearly understood why. I educated myself, being first drawn to books about Wicca and magic, then to self-help books and channeled material. This was the awareness I had needed all along! It gave me hope, and I knew all was well.

Even when I was alone in my room or home, I always felt that I was being watched—that every move and every moment was being judged and recorded on some tablet. So just "being," alone in the woods, was nice. This was one of the best techniques to balance and integrate all I felt, and help me find myself when I felt lost about who I was.

Another part of being an Indigo was feeling an incredible amount of anger and rage while growing up, because whenever I expressed how I felt, nobody could understand. This built up until finally I just stopped expressing myself. I felt I was on a different frequency and ready to explode from it. I would throw a chair, lash out and curse at someone, or just drink my anger away.

You see, I was "expanding," and since I was straying from the norm, I was given a pill to try to contain that. But I was in expansion and could never be controlled or contained. I was, and still am, constantly in expansion. *That's what it feels like to be an Indigo.*

One of the most incredible experiences I have ever had was the EMF Balancing Technique® by Peggy Dubro[89]—the rewiring of the body's electromagnetics at some level. After the first phase, I felt hugely different within myself, like night and day. It felt like every circuit in my body was completed. All the tiny roads in my body and my fields that still had road work on them were just completely finished and done. I felt very grounded, much more in control and balanced.

I felt peaceful and more able to contain myself and understand my emotions. I was able to release negative emotions. Bad moods would just pass, and then I would be fine. EMF balancing is pretty much common sense to me, and I feel every other Indigo should learn this technique. As a matter of fact, every other person on Earth should get this done if they want life to feel a bit more easy and if they want more control over their life.

One huge breakthrough came for me when I was introduced to a live essence food called super blue-green algae. After eating this for three days, my whole life started to change. It felt like circuits in my body were connecting, and I expanded to contain all of myself! I felt calm and in control—my concentration increased along with my energy levels and memory. I had a new sense of inner power and felt more calm and balanced than ever before. This food really saved my life. *I highly recommend it to any other Indigos.*

It is very important to me to spend time by myself. Alone, I become very open, like a flower. My special alone-time place is a nature center near me. When I go early in the morning, I step out of everyday life and can review it as a detached overview, as if it's a movie. Without this alone time, I can only see what is immediately around me, and I get confused and frustrated. In my solitude, I can see my life as a whole more clearly. I can more easily see why I am having a challenge in a certain area. I can see my path through the forest, and where it will take me if I continue to follow it. I can see the dead ends and where the foliage and brush need to be trimmed.

I also receive more loving insights about everything, especially myself. If something is irritating me, I can look at it without judgment. When I am with people, I interact just fine, but when I am alone something magical happens; my intuition is enhanced. I feel more in control of my life. Then I return to everyday life with a higher awareness, able to deal with life's situations.

I feel it is very important to honor people's space and their sacred private time. When I am alone in the woods, I can just be myself, and that is that. I can talk to the trees and everything around me, and they just listen and love me for who I am. It's nice to be in a place where I can just "be," where I know there is no chance of being judged by anybody. I grew up feeling very judged—very different.

If I had an Indigo Child, I would treat that person differently. I would immediately put her or him on high-vibration live-essence superfoods, especially blue-green algae, teach grounding techniques, and have this child EMF balanced. I would make sure they had self-awareness about their uniqueness, which is a gift—not wrong, bad, or evil.

I would probably not put them in school. Instead, I'd talk to other parents and form a group to teach the children about things they really need to know—about spirituality, who they really are, how to express themselves, how to release anger, and how to obtain self-worth, self-growth, self-love, love of others, and intuition. I myself was totally bored in school. None of it made sense, learning about studies of the past. I really did not care about the past. I was having trouble in the present, and the future seemed pretty dark.

The school system definitely needs to be restructured—it is ridiculous that an evolving human being should be treated like a little punk. We need to make sure that schoolteachers are properly trained and are balanced people. Plenty of unbalanced teachers take out a lot of "stuff" on children. The same problem occurs at psychiatric hospitals. Patients should be allowed to get connected to the earth instead of just given pills and kept separate from each other.

Indigos have a lot more tools to use in life. A non-Indigo may have a shovel to dig a hole with, while an Indigo has a tractor or a backhoe. So they can dig that hole faster, but also dig it very deep and fall into it very far. If they are unbalanced, they have no ladder to get out. So in a way Indigos can use their gifts against themselves.

Let us emphasize that Ryan did not get a "heads up" about this book. We solicited his comments because we had heard his story, but he was not coached. His story really was his own, as you can probably tell. He tells you about his "expansion," and that nobody can understand him, even when he tries to explain what is happening. This is classic Indigo. In addition, did you see his humanitarianism? In the mental ward, he became the helper to the others, who immediately picked up on this. He also stated, "I will overcome all of this and then show all the other children how to do the same. I know there is a way." His concern is to *identify* so that others can be helped as well. He intuitively knows that there are others like him.

He was constantly in the "now." He only focused on what "is," not what will be. This is also classic Indigo, and is one reason that they cannot see the consequences of their actions. The Christmas present–opening scenario; the candy store scenario; the desire to just "be"; the overwhelming desire to be alone—it all speaks of being in the "now." This is an expanded awareness for a child, something that often does not come until much later in life. He had it right away, and it was labeled as "weird." Ryan said, "I was, and still am, constantly in expansion. *That's what it feels like to be an Indigo.*"

Ryan could "read" people. He didn't say much about that since many still feel that this is weird. To us, it's just the ability to sense energy around people, and make intelligent decisions based on that. Some adults call it intuition. He had a good dose of it early, and was frustrated because he could "see" that his teachers and doctors were unbalanced! What a gift . . . but what an anchor if not understood.

Ryan felt evolved, but he felt that nobody knew it. Remember earlier when we told you that Indigo Children feel like royalty? Ryan said he "felt like a king working for a peasant, viewed as a slave." He is also bitter about school. What kind of travesty is it to have teachers who don't recognize who you are?

The references to super blue-green algae and the Dubro EMF Balancing Technique were revelations to us! We had no idea that Ryan was utilizing these resources. His comments sound like commercials—they must have helped him a great deal.

You might want to know that Ryan's parents survived all this, and today they have a loving son who is balanced, happy, settled, and their best friend. Honestly. If nothing else, that will tell you that there is hope for whoever it is in your life who seems to be hopeless. Never give up!

We received the following letter, short and sweet, from **Cathy Reiter,** another Indigo:

> I am 16 years old. I believe that I am enlightened and find it very frustrating to try to understand the actions, thoughts, and feelings of others my age. I have just met someone who shares my thoughts and is himself enlightened. I was so amazed to find somebody I have been looking for my whole life, who can share my experiences.
>
> I just read your chapter about Indigo Children and felt oddly relieved by the fact that there are other children and teenagers as frustrated as I am.
>
> I find that just writing this and being heard inspires me to believe that something could happen. Do you get much response from people my age? I don't know where to go next. I suppose I'll just go on with my life, and see where my path takes me.

Like Ryan's, this short note was received due to the small mention of Indigo Children in *Partnering with God,* my [Lee Carroll's] last book. Cathy doesn't say she is smart. She says "enlightened." She also found the Indigo information all by herself, while reading an adult self-help metaphysical book! She is also reaching out to see if anyone is "out there." Finally, she is very happy that she found another person her age who understands, since most her age do not. If Cathy is an Indigo (we think she is), then she must feel alone. Most Indigos are about six to ten years old. Cathy is another forerunner, as is the following Indigo contributor, **Candice Creelman**.

All You Need Is Love:
The Indigo Experience
Candice Creelman

From the beginning I knew that something was different about me, although I didn't know what. I remember my first day of kindergarten so clearly, walking into the group that was already situated around our teacher. I walked into the group and immediately knew that something was very strange and that I really didn't belong there. The other kids, from day one, literally began to treat me as though I was an alien or something. I don't remember what was specifically said by the other kids, but I remember being made to feel that I was unworthy of being in this group and that I didn't belong. This continued all through school to college, and then out into the "real" world.

School was a great struggle for me, not only because I was set apart and considered "different," but because I knew that most of the course work was total garbage and had nothing to do with the *real* world. I knew all along that I would never use anything they taught me, and no matter how hard people tried to convince me otherwise, I knew that what school taught was relatively useless. Outside of the basic reading, writing, and math skills, and having an idea of what's out there, they were just spewing useless information. Although I didn't fully know what this meant at the time, it's basically proven to be true for me. One thing that always bothered me as I got closer to graduating is that the only thing we were really taught was how to spew what they told us back to the teacher, how it was handed down and handed down without any reasoning or independent thought whatsoever. How was this going to help us in the real world?

So, given my frustration with school and the fact that I was bored silly with it, I didn't do very well. In fact, I was lucky to get through. I graduated high school with just above the minimum to get out of there, so I didn't have to deal with being ostracized by my peers anymore. However, that ended up continuing into my years in college, and to some extent it still continues today.

My parents, though they loved me dearly, just didn't have any clue what I was really, truly going through. I would hear things from my mom like, "Everyone gets picked on," and "Kids can be so cruel," and here's the best one, which now makes me laugh out loud: "Just ignore them and they'll leave you alone." Untrue—and so much easier said than done. Not only did they not leave me alone, but they would tease me more if I resorted to sitting in a corner cowering.

Instead of spending my childhood doing regular things, like hanging out with other kids, I spent my time in my mom and dad's basement with my music, which got me through all of this. This proved to be a very good thing, as music has become my career. Needless to say, I ended up with such low self-esteem that to this day, I still fight those old voices in my head that told me I was a loser and so on. I went to a retreat recently where I didn't feel like I belonged, and suddenly, I was right back in school. So those scars are still there. Fortunately, I've developed ways of going within to find out what's going on so that I can heal them properly now.

Right before I graduated from high school, I got brave one day and decided to ask someone why I got treated the way I did. I was outside my school in the small town of Alberta, just outside of Edmonton, and I saw a girl that I had gone to school with since day one. I looked at her and out of the blue, I got the courage to ask. Before I knew what was happening, the words were out: "You know how I've been treated so badly throughout the years, right?" She stared at me blankly, pretending not to know what I was talking about. When I pressed her, she mumbled agreement. "Why?" I asked. "What did I ever do to you people to deserve that? What could I have possibly done that would deserve such horrible treatment?"

She looked around, trying to get out of answering my question. When she realized she couldn't, she began to think about it. All she could come up with was, "Because you're different." At the time, all I could say or think was, "What are you talking about? What do you mean different? And even if I am, why should that cause people to do and say the things they've said all these years?"

At that time, I had no idea how or why I was different, but in the past few months I have begun to gain insight. I'm glad now that these experiences made me stronger, even though at the time it was horrifying. I spent my childhood and teen years feeling completely alone. I had no one that I could really relate to. Therefore, I moved to Toronto, on the other side of the country, for two and a half years. However, this past summer, I was "forced" to go back home to Edmonton because my mom was sick. It ended up being the best summer in my life, because I was able to finally put the past behind me.

At the very least, it gave me the ability to go within. Also, I found a group of people with whom I finally felt like I belonged. I had never once felt like I belonged anyplace. My friends gave me this, which in turn gave me a new sense of purpose and confidence. Now I'm learning not to hide the real me inside; the real me is very beautiful. Now that I'm back in Toronto again, I feel a great deal more whole within myself and far more empowered than ever before.

It was actually a difficult decision to go back, because I had never felt this strong sense of belonging. However, I also felt strongly that I had things to do here in Toronto. I'd learned that you can't run away from your ghosts. Sooner or later, you have to face yourself, as I did this summer in Edmonton. I learned a great deal about my past and what it really meant.

Becoming aware of the Indigo phenomenon also explained a lot for me and has helped me to better understand who and what I am and why I am here at this time. This has given me the power to heal all past hurts so that I can move on as an empowered, confident human being. I have chosen to put all this untapped energy into my music by writing about the really important things in life.

Many times I've encountered resistance when sharing with others how I felt "ahead" of most people—ahead of my time, to borrow a phrase. What I've learned, experienced, and felt is far beyond what most people can even remotely begin to understand. This has proven to be very frustrating and sometime devastating to me, mostly because when I've made the mistake of voicing this "knowing" to others who didn't understand, the response I've gotten is that I'm the one who really doesn't get it, that I'm too young to have that kind of wisdom, and that I'm being egotistical in saying I'm "beyond" someone with more experience in these matters.

Well, I'm here to say that physical experience has nothing to do with wisdom. Everyone, no matter what age, has access to this wisdom; it's whether you are open enough to allow it to come through—not how old you are—that counts.

That same summer, I grew spiritually in many ways. In my Master-level Reiki course, I knew I had zoomed way ahead of most people there, including those who had been practicing for many years. Before I even knew what it was, I did it all in one year. My mistake (or was it?) was to tell a lot of people about it. I knew that most of them were downright angry at me for talking about how far ahead I felt I was, and how the Reiki retreat was really just playtime for me. Several people tried to tell me that I had missed the subtleties of the retreat, but I knew I hadn't. I had enjoyed myself for the most part, but for me the stuff we talked about was pretty basic.

Of course, when I talk like this, people automatically assume that this is coming purely from the ego. I had the same experience with another teacher this summer who told me I was being egotistical. He came down on me pretty hard and really shot my confidence. However, all I know is what I know, and there's no way for me to prove what I know. I just do.

I don't feel that I make a big deal out of being Indigo— I'm only doing it now for the purpose of this book to help people understand what it's like. The Indigo thing just helps me understand what I've gone through—and continue to go through. In the past I considered it to be a burden; I hated being different. Now I rejoice in it because I understand it, and I can now call it an adventure. I wake up every morning feeling like a kid on Christmas, and I never thought I'd get that feeling back again. But here I am, loving every day. I'm alive and rejoicing in the wondrousness of it all. Everyone has access to what's out there, although Indigos seem to "get it" a lot sooner than most.

So, due to my experience, my best advice to those concerned with Indigos is to be *understanding*. Indigos simply and truly need your love and support, but we can't be healthy if you shove feelings of separation at us. We need to know that we are loved, supported, and important. Knowing this, we will have the power to be who we truly are, without being ashamed of being "different." I don't know how many times I wished for just one thing: for someone to tell me that they loved me and I was special. Not in a condescending way, but in an empowering way that would give me the feeling I had a great purpose here, as we all do.

We can't be helped by others pointing at us and saying, "Ooh, that's one of those Indigos. Wow! Let's put them on display." Please, instead let us know that it's really okay to be who we are, and just love us for that—who we *truly* are—that's it. Simply put, the song that describes it best is "All You Need Is Love"—true for everyone, not just Indigos. That song should be the theme for the planet right now, because love is all we're truly here to achieve—Heaven on Earth is more than just a childlike dream or imagination—the imagination is where it all begins. Heaven on Earth is a reality, although not everyone can see it yet. Indigos are part of the group who can see it. It's already here, so believe it and it is so!

Candice has some very basic things in common with Ryan, and with most Indigos. She is also in her mid-20s. Did you notice how bad she felt about feeling "different"? It really marked her to be separated out. You might also see a theme in her bitterness toward school. Believe us, this is going to mushroom—this rebellion to how education is presented. It's happening right now, according to many educators. Candice's differentness was really her "knowingness," her being more wise than most others, which prevented her from fitting in.

The other shared theme was the absolute knowledge that she was enlightened. She "knew" stuff that older, more experienced students were trying to learn. She floated through classes about ancient wisdom techniques as if she had always known them. This is another attribute of the Indigo kids. Just when you are trying to teach them something, they express boredom and want to go on the advanced level, or quit entirely. This may seem obstinate to you, but probably they have already grasped the subject matter—so why continue? It's not just intelligence—it's wisdom past their years. Candice's article is filled with evidence for this, and each time she tries to let us know that it's not ego—it just "is."

As with Ryan, her solace was to be alone. Alone, she was in control and could do as she wished at her own accelerated speed. It also shielded her from those who shunned her. Although she felt she was special, her peers and teachers beat her up verbally so that her self-worth was really tested. Even though Indigos come in feeling "expanded," as Ryan said, over time that very staple of their personality can be beat out of them. This was the case with both Ryan and Candice. Celebrate the fact that with balance, they got it back!

Both Indigos also felt that it was a mistake to have told others how they felt! It seemed to worsen the situation and caused them to be ostracized from their peer group. Yet they continued to try to tell others how they felt. In retrospect, both of them now feel that they should have just shut up and let the world find out who each of them were without their help. We simply can't imagine how difficult this must have been!

Look at this: Ryan, Cathy, and Candice all sought out spiritual wisdom *on their own*. As we have told you before, this is also something Indigos prefer to do. They will excel in church, since that is where love belongs. They are drawn to the universal principles of love because they understand them and feel "at home" around them.

What did Candice say was the key to her solace? Love. Most of the contributing Ph.D.'s and educators in this book said the same thing. Candice's desire to be loved and respected surpassed almost everything else. Her message to all of us? *Love the Indigo Children!*

chapter six

Summary

A Message from Jan Tober

In researching the Indigo Children, something became quite apparent to us: Even though these children are a relatively new group of beings, their ageless wisdom is showing us a new and more loving way to be—not just with them, but with each other.

Lee and I thought this was going to be a book about children, a book for parents, grandparents, teachers, and counselors. But it's really a book about *all* of us. These children ask us to drop words such as *guilt* and *victim* from our vocabulary and replace them with positive words such as *hope, compassion,* and *unconditional love.* None of this is new—the Little Ones are merely giving us the opportunity to practice, practice, practice.

They are offering us a new way to measure them, as well as ourselves. They wear their God-given gifts on their sleeves:

- They remind us to stay present and in the moment in *all* of our relationships.

- They ask us to be responsible for what we say and what we project, both consciously and subconsciously.

- They ask us to take responsibility for ourselves.

- These "royal beings" reflect the preciousness of each one of us. Are we not *all* royalty—all spiritual beings having a physical experience here on Earth?

Finally, there is one more exquisite gift from these Indigos. As we are learning to honor them and their process, and as we are learning to parent in a more effective way, we are also learning to honor and lovingly parent that profound Inner Child in each one of us. The Indigos ask us to play. If you don't have time for fun, make time! It must be created *by us*. It is not automatically given to us. If life becomes so serious that we cannot play, laugh, create a blanket fort on a rainy day, and run through the mud with the dog, then we're lost. A wise person once said, "It's not what we're given; it's what we do with it."

To conclude, let me share the following with you:

Children of the Light
For All Children . . .
Author Unknown

The time of the Great Awakening is come. You who have chosen to lift your eyes from darkness to the light are blessed to see the event of a new day on planet Earth. Because your heart has yearned to see real peace where war has reigned, to show mercy where cruelty has dominated, and to know love where fear has frozen hearts, you are privileged to your world.

Planet Earth is a blessing to you. She is your friend and your Mother. Always remember and honor your relationship with her. She is a living, loving, breathing being, like unto yourself. She feels the love that you give as you walk upon her soil with a happy heart.

The Creator has chosen your hands to reach the lonely, your eyes to see innocence not guilt, and your lips to utter words of comfort. Let pain be no more! You have wandered in dark dreams for so long now. Step into the light and send for what you know is truth. The world has suffered, not from evil, but from the fear of acknowledgment of the good. Allow the fear to be released now and forever—released into the light and transformed. It is within your power to do so.

No one can find yourself but you. All of your answers are within. Teach the lessons you have learned. Your understanding has been given, not only for yourself, but to guide a sore and tired world to a place of rest in a new consciousness.

Here before you is your vision come true. Here is your answer given you—a song to soothe a weary soul and make it new again. Here is the bridge that joins you to your brothers and sisters. Here is your Self. Look gently upon yourself, and allow yourself to be filled by the Light you have been seeing. True love comes from yourself, and every thought is a blessing to the entire Universe.

All areas of your life will be healed. You will shine with a golden splendor that speaks of the One who created you in wisdom and glory. The past will dissolve like a dark dream, and your joy will be so brilliant that you will have no recollection of the night.

Go forth and be a messenger of Hope. Point the way to healing by walking in gratefulness. Your brothers and sisters will follow. And as you pass beyond the portal of limitation, you will be united and reunited with all who seem to be lost. There is no loss in the Creator. Choose the path of forgiveness, and you will weep tears of joy for the goodness you find in all.

Go forth and live the life of the radiant soul that you are. Glorify the Creator in your every deed. You are important, you are needed, and you are worthy. Do not allow the dark cloak of fear to hide the light from your view. You were not born to fail. You are destined to succeed. The hope of the world has been planted in your breast, and you are assured of success as you stand for the One who Created you.

This, then, is the healing of Planet Earth. All your doubts and fears can be set aside, as you know the healing comes through the love in your heart.

A Message from Lee Carroll

The academic aspects of writing a book are now common to me—this is my seventh. What sets this one apart, however, is what lurks behind all these words you have read—the profound combined human experience of children in distress who created these thoughts and brought these ideas into view.

During seminars, we stand in receiving lines constantly so that attendees can meet and hug us—and spill out some of their troubles or joys. Parent after parent will come and tell us to please send energy to their son or daughter who they know to be Indigo, and who is confused or having great troubles in school. Teachers constantly ask, "What can I do?" Each case is different, but oddly similar. Day-care workers report that some of the children actually seem to be forming new paradigms of playing and new ways of treating each other that have not been seen before at these ages.

Nurses and caregivers who work with kids tell amazing stories about how the Indigos rally other needy children in places where life is very temporary. Our hearts cry when we hear the stories of what they do when kids are sick and dying. This is where Indigos shine, where nobody is there to make fun of them and tell them they are "too different." There are few adults around, and the other children are too weak to care. The Indigos will organize the games, give love to others far beyond their age, and even give counsel!

They lay next to the gravely ill and give them love and company, and then move on to others who are too tired or sick to wonder who those "weird" kids are. They do this until they themselves are too sick. Then, just like the others, they lie down. This is something we didn't go into in this book. It's too hard for some of us to look at and examine under those circumstances. It's a place most of us don't wish to go and see, but the nurses have to . . . and they tell us about the "new kind of child."

Indigos sometimes come to our seminars, and they stand in line, too. Sometimes they are as young as six, and they've asked their parents if they could attend with the grown-ups! One six-year-old boy could hardly wait to see if I "recognized" him. I told him I didn't—that we had never met. He winked and told me that he didn't really expect me to, but that I knew him before he was "him." He was a very old soul, and I still don't know what he knew, or thought he knew. Just the very idea that a six-year-old should have this concept is astounding. I don't care if he was only following another's ideology. It's the very idea of his eternalness and royalty that speaks to me. He believed it.

The teenage Indigos we speak to are very special. I wish I could get a bunch of them in a room together and we could just sing! I think they would love that. No phones, no typically teenage music or TV, but only a brief time for adults and teenagers to love each other. The teenagers have a message for us—I hear it all the time: "Age doesn't matter to us. We all *know* each other. If you will truly respect us, watch what we will do!"

These Indigo teenagers are very, very special. Each time I spend time with one, I walk away thinking, *I wasn't that way when I was 15! I just had a conversation with a wise adult in a very young body.* No wonder others think they're strange! The world has not seen this before, and it's probably very odd to some. Meanwhile, these are some of my favorite people on Earth, with a funny combination of the faddish goofiness of youth and the wisdom of the ages. It's an energy that you have to see to believe—like dressing in the latest garb, putting a ring in your upper lip, and listening to raucous rap music with your great-grandfather, a few priests, and a tribal medicine man—and having a great time!

The people who contributed to this book are fanatical about our kids. They have often "stepped over the line" in society to challenge a system or to take a stand for something that's unproven, but now they're being seen and identified. They are a very special bunch; they stick their necks out even to be in this book! Ask them, and they will tell you that the kids deserve it. They know it's time to get a consensus going in society that will build into a formidable group—a group that can recognize the attributes of an Indigo Child—and know exactly what to do.

Appendix

Contributor Biographies

(Numbers in parentheses refer to the pages where
the individual's contributions or services can be found.)

Karen Bolesky, M.A., C.M.H.C., L.M.P., is a Florida-licensed mental health counselor, and is also a certified Washington state mental health counselor. In addition, she is a licensed massage practitioner. Karen is represented in *Who's Who of American Women* and *Who's Who in Finance and Industry.*

She holds a bachelor of arts and a master of arts from the University of South Florida, and she currently serves as co-director and owner of the Soma Institute,[85] teaching neuromuscular integration. Karen has training in advanced gestalt techniques, bioenergetics, nutritional counseling, interpersonal process recall, counseling dying patients, advanced psychotherapy, and bio-kinetics. (195)

Contact information: The Soma Institute, 730 Klink St., Buckly, WA • (360) 829-1025 • www.soma-institute.com • *e-mail:* soma@nwrain.com

Candice Creelman contributed to chapter 5. She is one of the grown Indigos who volunteered to write a bit about her life for us to examine. She says, "All you need is love." (212)

Contact information: e-mail: amora@interlog.com

Barbra Dillenger, Ph.D., is a transpersonal development counselor who has worked in the metaphysical arena since 1969. She holds a minister's license and a B.A. and M.A. in education and psychology. She is also a doctor of metaphysical sciences. Barbra is known for her psychic and spiritual insights among those she works with. Her private practice is primarily composed of working professionals in many walks of life, and is centered in Del Mar, California; and San Francisco, California. (18)

Contact information: P.O. Box 2241, Del Mar, CA 92014

Peggy and Steve Dubro have been given a tremendous gift of universal knowledge. As members of the Kryon International Seminar team, they present life-empowering trainings all around the world that initiate individuals into a new awareness.

Peggy Phoenix Dubro cofounded The Energy Extension, Inc., of Norwich, Connecticut. She also channeled the Phoenix Factor information, which contained the EMF Balancing Technique.[89] Over the past seven years, Peggy has developed a unique understanding of the human energy field. This will be described in her upcoming book, *Spiritual Intelligence—The Gift of the Phoenix.* (199)

Contact information: Energy Extension, Inc., 624 W. Main St., #77, Norwich, CT 06360 • www.EMFBalancingTechnique.com

Karen Eck grew up in Baker City, Oregon. Always a seeker of the truth, her interest in health and science led her to move to Portland, Oregon, in 1970, where she attended Marylhurst College and St. Vincent School of Medical Technology. Karen has studied many healing modalities. Her conclusion—all types of healing occur primarily through one's belief in that system. Karen is currently a distributor of educational software, various learning programs, and nutritionals that have a track record of helping most medical conditions. She has just discovered the amazing properties of essential oils, and oil of wild oregano's ability to wipe out most infectious diseases and allergies. (179)

Contact information: 2499 8th St., Baker City, OR 97814
e-mail: kareneck@eoni.com • (541) 523-0494 • *website:* http://sky-family.com/wholisticare

Robert Gerard, Ph.D., is a lecturer, visionary, and healer. As a publisher, he owned and operated Oughten House Publications. Robert is the author of *Lady from Atlantis, The Corporate Mule,* and *Handling Verbal Confrontation: Take the Fear out of Facing Others.* He is currently touring and promoting his latest book, *DNA Healing Techniques: The How-To Book on DNA Expansion and Rejuvenation.* Robert offers workshops on DNA healing techniques. He is available for lectures and workshops worldwide. (37, 71)

Contact information: Oughten House Foundation, Inc., P.O. Box 1059, Coursegold, CA 93614 • *e-mail:* robert@oughtenhouse.com • www.oughtenhouse.com

Deborah Grossman graduated from Greenwich Academy in Connecticut. From there she attended Duke University in North Carolina, and then the University of Miami, where she obtained her nursing degree (BSN).

Deborah's passion is being a caregiver. She has taught for staff nurses in various medical disciplines, and at the School for Acupressure and Acupuncture in Miami until a few years ago. She now lectures in south Florida on topics such as self-care and introductory homeopathy. She is also a homeopathic nurse consultant, as well as the founder and president of Artemis International, a corporation dedicated to integrating all forms of healing. (185)

Contact information: 102 NE 2nd St., #133, Boca Raton, FL 33432

Debra Hegerle was initially a "left-brain" accountant for 14 years. She decided to follow a more "right brain" career path as a travel consultant by day and psychic reader by night. Six years later, she opened her own company, Dragonfly Productions, doing both bookkeeping and psychic consultancy.

She has been married for 16 years, has one child, and has been a volunteer teacher's aide for five years. Debra is a certified Reiki Master Teacher, student of astrology, and does Huna healing energy work. Other interests include horseback riding, jazz dance, and aerobics.

Debra currently volunteers for the San Francisco and San Jose branches of Compassion in Action, and has a long-term goal of starting a Compassion in Action in Contra Costa County, California. (32, 54)

Contact information: Dragonfly Productions, P.O. Box 2674, Martinez, CA 94553 • *e-mail:* daurelia@wenet.net

Ranae Johnson, Ph.D., is the author of *Reclaim Your Light Through the Miracle of Rapid Eye Technology.*[87] She has also written *Winter's Flower,* about raising an autistic child. Ranae has 7 children and 26 grandchildren and has founded the Rapid Eye Institute[88] in Oregon.

She attended Long Beach State in California and Brigham Young University. She became a doctor of clinical hypnotherapy at the American Institute of Hypnotherapy in Santa Ana, California, and obtained her Ph.D. at American Pacific University in Honolulu.

Ranae's list of certificates and training specialties are exceptional, with work in play therapy, grief counseling, time management, crisis management, advanced neurolinguistic programming, orthobionomy, and positive parenting, to name a few. She is a certified hypnotherapist with the National Guild of Hypnotists, and a Master NLP Technician. She is also a Master Rapid Eye Technician and trainer.

She has worked in Fountain Valley, California, with preschool autistic children; at The Community Mental Health Crisis Center in Spokane, Washington; with Parents of Autistic Children Support

Group in Spokane; and is currently maintaining the Rapid Eye Institute in Salem, Oregon. (196)

Contact information: Rapid Eye Institute, 3748 74th Ave., SE, Salem, OR 97301 • *e-mail:* ret.campus@aol.com • www.rapideyetechnology.com

Donna K. King is a graduate of the University of North Texas. She holds several certifications in biofeedback and neurofeedback. She is currently the Director of Professional Education at the Behavioral Physiology Institutes, a doctoral program in behavioral medicine in Bainbridge Island, Washington.

Ms. King has been actively involved in neurotherapy education, treatment, and research for both adults and children since 1992. She has been instrumental in developing biofeedback, neurofeedback, and related training programs that met the needs of clinicians in a variety of fields and backgrounds.

Ms. King also helped to develop summer camp neurotherapy programs for school-age children with ADD and ADHD. Since 1992, she has devoted the majority of her efforts toward the promotion and use of clinical behavioral medicine programs including neurotherapy. As an advisory board member of the Kidwell Foundation, Ms. King is working to make available state-of-the-art, comprehensive treatment programs to children nationwide from all walks of life. (191)

Contact information: 439 Bjune Rd. SE, Bainbridge Island, WA 98110 • *e-mail:* brainwm@aol.com

Ryan Maluski is one of the grown Indigos that volunteered to write a bit about his life for us to examine in chapter 5. He currently lives in Connecticut, and works in areas that specifically help others. Are you surprised? (202)

Contact information: Center for Synthesis, 31 Bridge Rd., Weston, CT 06883 • *e-mail:* Synthesis1@aol.com

Kathy A. McCloskey, Ph.D., Psy.D., spent almost ten years as a civilian U.S. Air Force scientist in Dayton, Ohio, conducting research on the effects of environmental stressors on human physiological and biomechanical performance. In her search for personal and professional meaning, she left the military to become a clinical psychologist. She received her second doctorate in August 1998, and is preparing to sit for the national board examination for independent licensure as a psychologist. She has successfully completed training in a crisis center, an inpatient hospital, a community mental health center, a university campus center, and a court-ordered batterers' treatment program.

Kathy has experience with diverse groups of people, including African-Americans, Appalachians, adolescents, children, gays, lesbians, bisexuals, the transgendered, battered women and their perpetrators, the campus community, and the severely mentally ill. She is presently employed as a postdoctoral fellow at the Ellis Human Development Institute in Dayton, Ohio. Her current specialties include brief crisis intervention therapy, treating court-ordered domestic violence perpetrators, existential approaches to life problems, and supervision of trainees.

Kathy belongs to the American Psychological Association, the Ohio Psychological Association, the American Association for the Advancement of Science, and the Human Factors and Ergonomics Society (HFES). She is the past chair of the HFES Test and Evaluation Technical Group, and is currently a nationally licensed Certified Professional Ergonomist. She has had numerous publications presented at annual meetings and in peer-reviewed journals, and has an extensive scientific publication record. She was also an adjunct professor of psychology at Wright State University from 1991 to 1994, and has been a clinical instructor at the Wright State

University School of Medicine since 1992. While obtaining her second doctorate, she was a tutor for courses within her program. Finally, she has been a licensed social worker for Ohio since 1996. (25)

Contact information: Ellis Human Development Institute, 9 N. Edwin C. Moses Blvd., Dayton, OH 45407 • *e-mail:* kcam@ gateway.net

Judith Spitler McKee, Ed.D., is a developmental psychologist, growth counselor, and professor emerita of educational psychology and early childhood education at Eastern Michigan University. She is the author of 12 textbooks on children's learning, development, play and creativity: *Play: Working Partner of Growth* (1986, ACEI); *The Developing Kindergarten* (MIAEYC, 1990), and ten volumes of *Annual Editions: Early Childhood Education* (1976–1991).

She conducts workshops for parents, teachers, librarians, therapists, and medical practitioners on children's development. She is also a nondenominational minister of the healing arts and a spiritual counselor. Working as a Seventh Degree Astarian and a Reiki master/teacher and Jin Shin practitioner, she writes for a series in *Healing Natural Alternatives* newsletter. She also conducts workshops on spiritual growth, holistic healing, and parenting Indigo Children. (56)

Contact information: Fax (248) 698-3961

Melanie Melvin, Ph.D., DHM, RSHom, has a doctorate in psychology and was licensed in California from 1988 to 1996. She has been licensed in Colorado since 1994 and is currently practicing there. She also has a diploma in homeopathic medicine, and belongs to the British Institute of Homeopathy and the North American Society of Homeopaths. She has been combining homeopathy with psychotherapy for her clients, including many children, for the past 18 years.

Melanie discovered homeopathy in 1970 after a car accident left her with numerous physical symptoms. For ten years she sought a doctor who would treat her whole person, instead of specializing. In 1980, a new acquaintance told her that there was such a doctor—a homeopath. Overjoyed, she went to see the homeopath began to heal, and started studying homeopathy. She felt she had come home, and has been working ever since with clients of all ages, combining her two disciplines. (112)

Contact information: 34861 W. Pine Ridge Lane, Golden, CO 80403 • (303) 642-9360 • *e-mail:* cmelwolf@aol.com • www. dmelanie.com

Robert P. Ocker is a middle-school guidance counselor in Mondovi, Wisconsin. His passion and purpose has been guiding youth; he has worked in the Eau Claire School District as an elementary school counselor, and implemented the CHAMPS Peer Leadership Training Program. In Lake Geneva, he worked as an elementary and middle-school counselor. He has given numerous presentations to audiences of all ages on "Education through Entertainment." Through drama, Robert helps students focus on problem solving, conflict resolution, student responsibility, and character education. He was recognized by the Wisconsin School Counselors Association as one of the most outstanding future educational leaders. He is a public speaker.

Robert is a certified preschool through 12th-grade counselor, holding a bachelor of arts in communication from the University of Wisconsin, Eau Claire, where he was recognized for his outstanding leadership and communication skills. He has studied, lived, traveled, and spoken throughout Europe. He also holds a master's of science in guidance and counseling from the University of Wisconsin, Stout. The graduate college honored Robert for his outstanding research, thesis, and educational vision.

He is a sincere, kind, caring, and energetic young man who shares his gifts with children and adults alike. (88, 123)

Contact information: 7717 35th Ave., Knolsha, WI 53142 • (715) 831-9429

Jennifer Palmer has a diploma in teaching (secondary, fine arts), and a bachelor's degree in education. She also holds a graduate certificate in education for professional practice. She has taught in public primary schools for 23 years in Australia. She is the recipient of the Advanced Skills Teachers Award and currently resides in Adelaide. (93)

Contact information: Jennifer is now in Australia. Feel free to e-mail her at kryonmail@aol.com, and your message will be forwarded. Indicate "Indigo book—Jennifer Palmer."

Cathy Patterson is a special education teacher in Vancouver, British Columbia, Canada. She works specifically with students who have severe behavior disorders, collaborating with various professionals to implement behavioral as well as academic plans.

Currently she is completing her master's in counseling psychology. She leads parenting group sessions in order to help support parents with challenging children. Cathy's most immediate goal is to help school professionals and families work together to meet the needs of children with behavioral difficulties within the public education system. (77)

Contact information: e-mail: rpatter262@aol.com

Rev. Laurie Joy Pinkham, D.D., "Owl Woman," lives in rural New England, where she continues to write and help people understand who they are and why they are here. She is an emissary of light, a healer, writer, and photographer. She hosts events around the country with the desire to bring spiritual awareness to the world. She is a catalyst for humankind, holding energy and building bridges in consciousness around the world. She writes about her own experiences in this life and in others, and does interviews about other's journeys that have appeared in publications around the world. Some of her lyrics from "Songs from God" have been recorded, and her stories, poems, interviews, and photography have appeared in magazines and newspapers around the globe. She is a Reiki Master, craniosacral therapist, and intuitive, and she holds a degree in early childhood education from the University of New Hampshire, as well as a doctorate of divinity. She is currently in private practice and has a chiropractic office in rural New England. (142)

Contact information: PMB #622, 67 Emerald St., Keene, NH 03431 • *e-mail:* owlwoman33@aol.com • www.owlwoman.com • (603) 526-8424

Pauline Rogers has been in child development all her life, and she consults in that field. She has a B.A. from California State University, and a master's in educational administration from the University of La Verne, in California. She has also taken courses in child development administration at the UCLA campus. She is the former head teacher and supervisor for Bellflower, California (eight sites), and was Child Development Program Coordinator for social services in Norwalk, California. She holds too many professional distinctions and memberships to list here. (103)

Contact information: 680 Juniper Way, La Habra, CA 90631

Richard Seigle, M.D., has a private practice in Carlsbad, California. He trained at UCLA and received his degree from USC.

Richard worked for three years on the Navajo reservation prior to completing his psychiatry residency at the University of California at San Diego (UCSD). Since then he has studied with many healers and teachers at the UCSD School of Medicine. (3)

Contact information: (760) 434-9778

Joyce Golden Seyburn has a B.S. in education from Wayne State University, and taught kindergarten and first grade. While her three children were young, she worked on her master's in early childhood development. A columnist for *The Detroit News*, Joyce has also been published in various magazines and has contributed to an anthology of short stories.

Her tenure at Deepak Chopra's Center for Mind/Body Medicine in La Jolla, California, spurred her interest in the subject of the mind/body connection. When she found herself about to become a grandmother for the first time and could not find any books on mind/body parenting to share with her children, she decided to write the first: *Seven Secrets to Raising a Happy and Healthy Child.*[56](104)

Contact information: 1155 Camino Del Mar, #464, Del Mar, CA 92014 • *e-mail:* joy7secrets@hotmail.com

Keith R. Smith is originally a graduate of San Francisco State College. His academic training, however, continued for another 20 years! He is a master herbologist (Dominion Herbal College in Canada and Christopher School of Natural Healing). He studied advanced iridology and took instructor training from Dr. Bernard Jenson. Keith is also an honors graduate from the School of Natural Health in Spanish Forks, Utah; and also studied at the School of Healing Arts in San Diego, California.

Along the way Keith became a master nutritionist and developed an interest in Rayid, which is the emotional-spiritual practice of iridology founded by Denny Ray Johnson. Keith is now president of the International Rayid Society, and is also a Rayid Master. He has practiced herbal medicine for 21 years, and you can find him in Escondido, California.[70](165)

Contact information: 360 N. Midway, Suite 102, Escondido, CA 92027 • *e-mail:* ksmithhrb@adnc.com • www.health-forum.com

Nancy Ann Tappe has been working in the field of parapsychology for 25 years. She majored in theology and philosophy in college and is an ordained minister. She is known throughout the U.S.A., Canada, and parts of Europe and Asia for her candid view of people and how we can better understand ourselves and others.

She began her studies in color and the human aura during her exploration of humanity. For three years she worked on defining and interpreting the aura itself, and quickly found that she had the rare gift of "seeing" auras—and was fanatical about somehow making sense of it.

To test the information she was intuitively getting, she contacted a psychiatrist in San Diego. With his cooperation, hundreds of patients and volunteers were tested, using the theory she was receiving. They worked for nine years until she was convinced she was accurate.

Nancy Ann then taught at San Diego State University in the experimental college. Today she continues lecturing, teaching, and counseling throughout the world.[2] (6, 47, 126)

Contact information: Starling Publishers, P.O. Box 278, Carlsbad, CA 92018

Doreen Virtue, Ph.D., holds bachelor's, master's, and doctoral degrees in counseling psychology. A frequent lecturer, she has written 12 books, with half a million copies in print worldwide, including *The Lightworker's Way* (Hay House, 1997), *Angel Therapy* (Hay House, 1997), and *Divine Guidance* (Renaissance/St. Martin's, August 1998). She also has created two audiocassettes, *Chakra Clearing* and *Healing with the Angels* (Hay House). Dr. Virtue's website at **www.angeltherapy.com** contains information about her workshops and books, and it has a very active message board.

The daughter of a Christian Science healer, Dr. Virtue is a fourth-generation metaphysician who blends psychic phenomena, angelic healing, psychology, and *Course in Miracles* spiritual principles into her counseling practice and writing. Her 12 years of clinical experience include serving as founder and director of an all-woman psychiatric hospital, directing an adolescent psychiatric program, and practicing private psychotherapy. In addition, Dr. Virtue is a faculty member of the American Institute of Hypnotherapy, where she teaches classes on psychic and mediumship development.

She co-organized several global peace prayers along with James Twyman and Gregg Braden. A frequent talk show guest, Virtue has appeared on *Oprah, Good Morning America, The View, Donahue, Ricki Lake, Geraldo, Sally Jessy Raphael, Montel, Leeza, The 700 Club, Gordon Elliott, CNN, Extra,* and others. She has given workshops about spirituality and mental health since 1989, and her audiences include The Whole Life Expo, The Universal Lightworker's Conference, The Health and Life Enrichment Expo, Fortune 500 companies, The Learning Annex, and The American Board of Hypnotherapy convention. (23, 51, 132, 156)

Contact information: www.AngelTherapy.com, or through Hay House Publicity, P.O. Box 5100, Carlsbad, CA 92018-5100

ENdNotes

1.   Gibbs, Nancy. "The Age of Ritalin." *Time* magazine, page 86. November 30, 1998.

2.   Tappe, Nancy Ann. *Understanding Your Life Through Color.* 1982. ISBN 0-940399-00-8. Starling Publishers, PO Box 278, Carlsbad, CA 92018. This book is not widely distributed. To obtain, call Awakenings Book Store (credit cards accepted) in California at (949) 457-0797 or email to govinda4u@aol.com • Mind, Body, Soul Bookstore in Indiana at (317) 889-3612 or e-mail to mndbodsoul@aol.com

3.   Taylor, Hartman, Ph.D. *The Color Code: A New Way to See Yourself, Your Relationships, and Life.* 1998. ISBN 0684843765. Scribner.

4.   *The Rising Curve: Long-Term Gains in IQ & Related Measures,* edited by Ulric Neisser and published by the American Psychological Association, Washington, DC (1998). To order, call in the U.S.A. (800) 374-2721.

5.   Dr. Doreen Virtue references for all three sections in this book:
      Internet address [http://www.angeltherapy.com].
   "Ritalin use is a bar to military service." *Cox News Service.* Dec. 1, 1996.
   "A Course in Miracles," workbook lesson 198, 9.5. *Foundation for Inner Peace.* 1975.
   Hayes, Laurie L. "Ritalin use has doubled in past five years," *Counseling Today,* vol. 39, no. 11. May 1997.
   Kilcarr, P., and P. Quinn. "Voices from Fatherhood: Fathers, Sons and ADHD." 1997. New York: Brunner/Mazel, Inc.
   Lang, John. "Boys on Drugs." Scripps Howard News Service.

Schachar, R. J., R. Tannock, C. Cunningham, and P. Corkum. "Behavioral, Situational, and Temporal Effects of Treatment of ADHD with Methylphenidate." *Journal of the American Academy of Child and Adolescent Psychiatry,* 1997, 36(6):754-763.

6. The National Foundation for Gifted and Creative Children can be contacted by e-mail at <nfgcc@aol.com> or by writing to them at 395 Diamond Hill Road, Warwick, RI 02886; or call (401) 738-0937.

7. Wright, Robert. "The Power of Their Peers." *Time* magazine, p. 67, August 24, 1998.

8. Harris, Judith Rich. *The Nurture Assumption: Why Children Turn Out the Way They Do.* ISBN 0684844095. 480 pp. 1998. Free Press.

9. Bodenhamer, Gregory. *Back in Control—How to Get Your Children to Behave.* ISBN 0-671- 76165-X. 1988. Fireside, NY.

10. Millman, Dan. *The Life You Were Born to Live—A Guide to Finding Your Life Purpose.* ISBN 0915811-60-X. 1993. HJ Kramer, Inc.

11. Gomi, Taro. *Everyone Poops.* ISBN 0-916291-45-6. 1993. Brooklyn , NY: Kane/Miller Pub.

12. Baer, Edith. *This Is the Way We Eat Our Lunch.* ISBN 0590468871. 1995. NY: Scholastic.

13. Dooley, Norah. *Everybody Cooks Rice.* ISBN 0876144121. 1991. Minneapolis, MN: Caroliheda Books.

14. Gardner, Howard. *Frames of Mind: The Theory of Multiple Intelligences.* ISBN 046501822. 1983. NY: Basic Books.
McKee, Judith Spitler. *The Developing Kindergarten.* ISBN 0962915408. 1990. East Lansing, MI: Michigan Association for Education of Young Children.
Armstrong, Thomas. *Seven Kinds of Smarts: Discovering and Using Your Natural Intelligences.* ISBN 0452268192. 1993. NY: Plume/Penguin.

15. Erikson, Erik H. *Childhood and Society.* ISBN 039331068X. 1993. NY: Norton.

16. McKee, Judith Spitler. *Play: The Working Partner of Growth.* ISBN 0871731126. 1986. Olney, MD: Association for Childhood Education International.

17. Brown, Margaret Wise. *Goodnight Moon.* ISBN 0-064430170. NY: Harper Collins. 1947, reissued 1991.

18. Degan, Bruce: *Jamberry.* ISBN 0060214163.NY: Harper Collins. 1990.

19. Boynton, Sandra. *Barnyard Dance.* ISBN 1-563054426. 1993. NY: Workman Publishing.

20. Porter-Gaylord, Laurel. *I Love My Mommy Because. . . .* ISBN 0525446257. 1996. NY: Dutton.

21. Porter-Gaylord, Laurel. *I Love My Daddy Because. . . .* ISBN 0525446249. 1996. NY: Dutton.

22. Potter, Beatrix. *The Tale of Peter Rabbit.* ISBN 0590411012. 1987. NY: Scholastic.

23. Wescott, Nadine. *The Lady With The Alligator Purse.* ISBN 031693165. 1990. NY: Little Brown & Co.

24. Preston, Edna Mitchell. *The Temper Tantrum Book.* ISBN 0140501819. 1976. NY: Viking.

25. Piper, Watty. *The Little Engine That Could.* ISBN 0448400413. 1990. NY: Price/Stern/Sloan Publishers.

26. Raffi. *Baby Beluga* (Audiocassette). ISBN 6301878949. 1990. Universal City, CA: Rounder Records.

27. Ives, Burl. *Burl Ives: A Twinkle in Your Eye* (Audiocassette). ISBN 6304902158. 1998. Sony Wonder.

28. Milne, A.A. *Winnie the Pooh* (Audiocassette). Read by Charles Kuralt. ISBN 0140866825. 1997. Penguin Audio Books.

29. Rosenbloom, Joseph. *Doctor Knock Knocks.* ISBN 080698936X. 1976. NY: Sterling.

30. Rosenbloom, Joseph. *Biggest Riddlebook in the World.* ISBN 0806988843. 1976. NY: Sterling.

31. Hall, Katy, and Lisa Eisenberg. *101 Cat and Dog Jokes.* ISBN 0590433369. 1990. NY: Scholastic. *Note:* Katy Hall has many, many joke books!

32. Berenstain, Stan and Jan. *The Berenstain Bears and The Messy Room.* ISBN 0394856392. 1983. NY: Random House.

33. Berenstain, Stan and Jan. *The Berenstain Bears and Too Much TV.* ISBN 0394865707. 1984. NY: Random House.

34. Berenstain, Stan and Jan. *The Berenstain Bears and Too Much Junk Food.* ISBN 0394872177. 1985. NY: Random House.

35. White, E. B. *Charlotte's Web.* ISBN 0064400557. 1974. NY: Harper Trophy.

36. White, E. B. *Charlotte's Web* (Audiocassette). ISBN 0553470485. 1992. NY: Bantam Books Audio.

37. Herriot, James. *James Herriot's Treasury for Children.* ISBN 0312085125. 1992. NY: St. Martin's Press.

38. Kindersley, Barnabas and Anabel. *Children Just Like Me.* ISBN 078940217. 1995. NY: Dorling Kindersley and the United Nations Children's Fund.

39. Hoberman, Mary Ann. *Fathers, Mothers, Sisters, Brothers: A Collection of Family Poems.* ISBN 014054891. NY: Puffin/Penguin.

40. Baum, L. Frank. *The Wizard of Oz.* ISBN 067941794X. 1992. NY: Knopf. *Note:* Other Oz books include *Ozma of Oz, The Emerald City of Oz,* and *The Patchwork Girl of Oz.*

41. Cleary, Beverly. *Ramona Forever* (Audiocassette). Read by Stockard Channing. ISBN 0807272655. 1989. Old Greenwich, CT: Listening Library.

42. Lofting, Hugh. *The Story of Dr. Doolittle* (Audiocassette). Read by Alan Bennett. ISBN 0553477692. NY: Bantam Books Audio.

43. Rosen, Michael. *Walking the Bridge of Your Nose.* ISBN 1856975967. 1995. NY: Kingfisher.

44. Krull, Kathleen. *Lives of the Musicians (and What the Neighbors Thought).* ISBN 0152480102. 1993. San Diego, CA: Harcourt Brace.
————. *Lives of the Writers (and What the Neighbors Thought).* ISBN 0152480099. 1994. San Diego, CA: Harcourt Brace.
————. *Lives of the Artists (and What the Neighbors Thought).* ISBN 0152001034. 1995. San Diego, CA: Harcourt Brace.
————. *Lives of the Athletes (and What the Neighbors Thought).* ISBN 0152008063. 1997. San Diego, CA: Harcourt Brace.

45. L'Engle, Madeleine. *A Wrinkle in Time* (Audiocassette). ISBN 0788701371. 1994. Prince Frederick, MD: Recorded Books.

46. *Parenting with Love and Logic.* Contact Cline-Fay Institute, Inc.; 2207 Jackson Street; Golden, Colorado 80401. (800) 338-4065.

47. McArthur, David. "Learning to Love."*Venture Inward* magazine, page 33, January/February 1998.

48. McArthur, Bruce and David. *The Intelligent Heart.* 224 pp. ISBN 087604-389-9. A.R.E. Press.

49. Planetary LLC, publishers of the HeartMath® System: 14700 West Park Avenue, Boulder Creek, CA 95006. Toll free: (800) 372-3100. [http://www.planetarypub.com]. Deborah Rozman, Ph.D., Executive Director.

50. Childre, Doc Lew. *Freeze-Frame: One Minute Stress Management.* ISBN 1-879052-42-3.
————. *A Parenting Manual.* 160 pp. ISBN 1-879052-32-6.
————. *Teen Self Discovery.* 120 pp. ISBN 1-879052-36-9;
————. *Teaching Children to Love.* 80 games & fun activities for raising balanced children in unbalanced times. ISBN 1-879052-26-1.
To order any of the above, call Planetary LLC: (800) 372-3100.

51. Gregson, Bob. *The Incredible Indoor Games Book.* ISBN 0-8224-0765-5. Belmont, CA: David S. Lake Publishers.

52. Gregson, Bob. *The Outrageous Outdoor Games Book.*
    ISBN 0-8224-5099-2. Belmont, CA: David S. Lake Publishers.

53. Rozman, Deborah. *Meditating with Children.* ISBN 1-879052-24-5.
    Planetary LLC.

54. Goelitz, Jeffrey. *The Ultimate Kid.* Concerns holistic education. 154 pp.
    ISBN 0-916438-61- 9. Planetary LLC.

55. Herzog, Stephanie. *Joy in the Classroom.* ISBN 0-916438-46-5.
    Planetary LLC.

56. Seyburn, Joyce. *Seven Secrets to Raising a Happy and Healthy Child:
    The Mind/Body Approach to Parenting.* 1998. ISBN 0-425-16166-8.
    Berkley Press.

57. Drummond, Tammerlin. "Touch Early and Often." *Time* magazine,
    page 54, July 27, 1998.

58. Hallowell, Edward, M.D. *Driven to Distraction: Recognizing and Coping
    with ADD From Children Through Adults.* ISBN 0684801280. 1995.
    Simon and Schuster.

59. Taylor, John F. *Helping Your Hyperactive ADD Child.* ISBN 0761508686.
    Prima Publishing,1997.

60. Kurcinka, Mary Sheedy. *Raising Your Spirited Child: A Guide for Parents
    Whose Child is More Intense, Sensitive, Perceptive, Persistent, and
    Energetic.* ISBN 006092328-8. 1992. Harperperennial Library.

61. Sears, William, M.D., and Lynda Thompson, Ph.D. *The A.D.D. Book,
    New Understandings, New Approaches to Parenting Your Child.* 1994.
    ISBN 0-316-77873-7. [http://www.littlebrown.com]

62. Diller, Lawrence H. *Running on Ritalin: A Physician Reflects on Children,
    Society, and Performance in a Pill.* ISBN 0553106562. 1998.
    Bantam-Doubleday-Dell.

63. Block, Mary Ann. *No More Ritalin: Treating ADHD Without Drugs.*
    ISBN 1575662396. 1997. Kensington Publication Corp.

64. Beal, Eileen. *Ritalin: Its Use and Abuse.* ISBN 082392775X. 1999. Rosen Publishing Group.

65. CH.A.D.D. collects, organizes, and shares information on ADHD for doctors, schools, support groups, and parents. National: 499 Northwest 70th Avenue, Suite 101; Plantation, FL 33317; (800) 233-4050; Fax (954) 587-4599; [http://www.chadd.org]

66. Network of Hope: Mary Votel, Director. PO Box 701534, St. Cloud, FL 34770-1534. [http://www.networkofhope.org]. Fax: (407) 892-5657.

67. Barkley, R. *Hyperactive Children: A Handbook For Diagnosis and Treatment,* p. 13. 1981. New York: Guilford Press.

68. Breggin, Peter R., M.D. *Talking Back to Ritalin: What Doctors Aren't Telling You About Stimulants for Children.* ISBN 1567511295. 1998. Monroe, ME: Common Courage Press.
Breggin, Peter and Ginger. *Journal of College Student Psychotherapy,* Vol. 10 (2).1995.

69. Mendelsohn, Robert, M.D. *How to Raise a Healthy Child . . . in Spite of Your Doctor.* ISBN 0-345-34276-3.1984. Ballantine Books.

70. Keith Smith: E-mail at <ksmthhrb@adnc.com> or call the Herb Shop at (760) 489-6889. A website is in development with new information as this book is written: [http://www.health-forum.com]. Private consultations are available, with emergency appointments taken on a case-by-case basis per availability. Research references:
Lyon G. R., D. B. Gray, J. F. Kavanagh, et al (eds.). *Better Understanding Learning Disabilities: New Views from Research and Their Implications for Education and Public Policies.* Baltimore: Brookes, 1993.
Moats, L. C., and G. R. Lyon. *Learning Disabilities in the United States: Advocacy, Science, and the Future of the Field.* J Learn Disab 1993 26:282-294.
Stanovich, K. E., and L. S. Siegel. *Phenotypic Performance Profile of Children with Reading Disabilities: A Regression-Based Test of the Phonological-Core Variable-Difference Model.* J. Ed Psych 1994; 86:24-53.
Lyon, G. R. (ed.). *Frames of Reference for the Assessment of Learning Disabilities: New Views on Measurement Issues.* Baltimore: Brookes, 1994.

Duane, Drake D., and David B. Gray. *The Reading Brain: The Biological Basis of Dyslexia.* ISBN 0912752254. 1991. Parkton, MD: York.

National Advisory Committee on Handicapped Children: Special Education for Handicapped Children. Washington, DC: Department of Health, Education and Welfare, 1968.

Lyon, G. R. *Research in Learning Disabilities* (tech. report). Bethesda, MD: National Institute of Child Health and Human Development, 1991.

A Guide to Medical Cures and Treatments—A Complete A to Z Sourcebook of Medical Treatments, Alternative Options and Home Remedies. P. 237, "Inattention/Hyperactivity Comparison." ISBN 0895778467. A Reader's Digest Book publication, 1996.

71. Research in Learning Disabilities at the NICHD (National Institute of Child Health and Human Development) by G. Reid Lyon, Ph.D. Human Learning and Behavior Branch, Center for Research for Mothers and Children—with contributions from scientists supported by: National Institute of Child Health and Human Development, National Institutes of Health. LD.htm at [http://www.nih.gov], page 1.

72. Ibid., page 9.

73. [http://www.mediconsult.com] *Attention Deficit Disorder News* and *Attention Deficit Hyperactivity Disorder.* Deca. p. 1, paragraph 5, summary: p. 10 of 11, paragraph 2.

74. Insight USA: 1771 S. 350 E., Provo, UT 84606. (801) 356-1322. [http://www.insight-usa.com]. E-mail to Karen Eck: <kareneck@worldnet.att.net>

75. Nutri-Chem: 1303 Richmond Rd.; Ottawa, Ontario, K2B 7Y4, Canada; Toll Free 1-888-384- 7855 (Canada and U.S.A.). [http://www.nutrichem.com]

76. "Doctors Give Alternative Remedies Closer Look." Associated Press quoted in *Norwich Bulletin: Health,* November 11, 1998. Reporting on *The Journal of the American Medical Association*; Book 008, November 11, 1998 (alternative medicine edition).

77. Taylor, John F. *Answers to ADD: The School Success Tool Kit.* 102-minute video with over 125 techniques described and illustrated. ISBN 1-883963-00-1. [http://www.add-plus.com/video.html]

78. *Network of Hope* newsletter, February 1998, nutrition edition.
P.O. Box 701534, St. Cloud, FL 34770.

79. Cell Tech: 1300 Main Street, Klamath Falls, OR 97601. (800) 800-1300.
[http://www.celltech.com] The following people understand Indigos and
will explain the blue-green product. Distributor: L. Askey, (250) 342-7162
or <lyaskey@rockies.net> Distributors: Michael & Sandy Lansdale at
(800) 342-9548 or mlansdale@aol.com. You can contact John Paino at
(978) 371-2355, paino@earthlink.net [http://www.the-peoples.net/celltech]

80. Lawrence, Ron, M.D., Ph.D., Paul Rosch, M.D., F.A.C.P., and Judith
Plowden. *Magnetic Therapy: The Pain Cure Alternative.*
ISBN 0-7615-1547-X. CA: Prima Publishing,
[http://www.primapublishing.com]

81. Neurotherapy training: Behavioral Physiology Institutes, 175 Parfitt Way,
Suite N150; Bainbridge Island, WA 98110. (206) 780-5500 ext. 104.
[http://www.bp.edu]. E-mail: <proed@bc.edu>

82. Neurotherapy treatment facilities: Kidwell Institute, 1215 Mulberry Lane,
Oklahoma City, OK 73116. (405) 755-8811.
[http://www.kidwellinstitute.com]. E-mail: <kidwell@theshop.net>

83. Lubar, J. F., and M. N. Shouse. "The Use of Biofeedback in the
Treatment of Seizure Disorders and Hyperactivity." *Advances in
Child Clinical Psychology,* 1, pp. 204–251. Plenum Publishing
Company.
Lubar, J. O., and J. F. Lubar. "Electroencephalographic Biofeedback of
SMR and Beta for Treatment of Attention Deficit Disorders in a
Clinical Setting." *Biofeedback and SelfRegulation,* 9, pp. 1–23.
Mann, C. A., J. F. Lubar, A.W. Zimmerman, B. A. Miller, and R. A.
Muenchen. "Quantitative Analysis of EEG in Boys with Attention
Deficit/Hyperactivity Disorder (ADHD)—A Controlled Study with
Clinical Implications." *Pediatric Neurology,* 8, pp. 30–36.

84. The Focus Neuro-Feedback Training Center: 2101 Business Center Drive,
Suite 120; Irvine, CA 92612. (714) 833-1882.

85. The Soma Institute of Neuromuscular Integration: 730 Klink, Buckly, WA
98321. (360) 829-1025. [http://www.soma-institute.com]

86. Dr. Sid Wolf, H.H.P., Ph. D.; Phoenix Healing Center (nationally certified in therapeutic massage and body work). 1017 Vision Way, Lyons, CO 80540. (303) 823-5873.

87. Johnson, Ranae, Ph.D. *Rapid Eye Technology* and *Winter Flower.* Books available on the website: [http://www.rapideyetechnology.com]

88. Rapid Eye Institute: 3748 74th Ave. SE; Salem, OR 97301. (503) 373-3606. [http://www.rapideyetechnology.com]

89. Peggy and Steve Dubro. The EMF Balance Technique: Phoenix Factor. [http://www.EMFBalancingTechnique.com]

About the Authors

Jan Tober and Lee Carroll speak worldwide before thousands of seminar attendees on human enablement and empowerment. Lee has authored eight self-help books over the past ten years, which have been translated into multiple languages. Jan and Lee have been invited three times to present their messages of hope and love at the United Nations in New York City, the last time being in November of 1998.

❖ NOTES ❖

NOTES

NOTES

We hope you enjoyed this Hay House book.
If you would like to receive a free catalog
featuring additional Hay House books and products,
or if you would like information about the
Hay Foundation, please contact:

Hay House, Inc.
P.O. Box 5100
Carlsbad, CA 92018-5100

(760) 431-7695 or **(800) 654-5126**
(760) 431-6948 (fax) or **(800) 650-5115 (fax)**

Please visit the Hay House website at: **www.hayhouse.com**